GARDEN CONIFERS IN COLOUR

Garden Conifers

in Colour

Brian and Valerie Proudley

BLANDFORD PRESS
POOLE   DORSET

First published in 1976 by Blandford Press,
Link House, West Street, Poole, Dorset BH 15 1LL
Copyright © Blandford Press Ltd.

Reprinted 1984

ISBN 0 7137 1458 1

Printed and bound in Hong Kong by South China Printing Co.

CONTENTS

Acknowledgements 6

Introduction 7

1 The conifers and their names 12

2 Conifers in the garden 19

3 How to grow them 28

4 Propagation 37

5 Troubles 47

6 Growth rate and ultimate size 51

The colour plates 55

Descriptions 121

Appendix: Check-list of Conifer Families and Genera . 203

Glossary of botanical and gardening terms . . . 205

Select bibliography 207

Index of plants described 209

ACKNOWLEDGEMENTS

We wish to express our thanks to the owners of the following arboreta, gardens and nurseries for their kind assistance in allowing us to photograph the specimens depicted in the colour plates.

Arboreta and gardens
Arboretum Kalmthout, Belgium (M R. de Belder); Botanical Gardens, Gisborne, New Zealand; Proefstation voor de Boomkwekerij, Boskoop, Holland (The Director); Private garden, Moore Street, Leamington, Cambridge, New Zealand (Mr and Mrs Bellingham); Great Comp, Borough Green, Sevenoaks, Kent (Mr and Mrs R. Cameron); Savill and Valley Gardens, The Great Park, Windsor, Berkshire (The Crown Estate Commissioners); Von Gimborn Arboretum, Doorn, Holland (University of Utrecht); Wisley Garden, Ripley, Surrey (The Royal Horticultural Society).

Nurseries
Bridgemere Nursery, Woore, Cheshire (Mr John Ravenscroft); Messrs Duncan and Davies, New Plymouth, New Zealand; Messrs Hillier and Sons, Jermyns Gardens and Arboretum, Romsey, Hampshire; Messrs Ingwersen, Birch Farm Nursery, Gravetye, near East Grinstead, Sussex; Mr George Osmond, Archfield Nursery, Wickwar, Gloucestershire; Messrs Robinsons, Knockholt, Kent (and also Mrs Robinson's private garden); The Wansdyke Nursery and Pygmy Pinetum, Hillworth Road, Devizes, Wiltshire.

All of the above firms can be recommended as suppliers of high quality conifers; some offer export facilities. Each issues a catalogue annually.

Special thanks are due to Mr H. G. Welch of Devizes for advice on the nomenclature (we should add that any mistakes that may have occurred are our responsibility).

INTRODUCTION

Most people, even if only remotely interested in the living world, should know what conifers are, for they are among the most frequently seen trees over almost all the temperate regions of the world. Each of the different kinds may not be known by name, but as a group many are known by sight by the obvious fact that most bear cones—a guide to their identity. This feature prompted the title conifer: it is a compound Latin word derived from *conus* 'a cone' and *fero* 'bearing'. However, not all conifers have these cones and the seeds of junipers are found within a berry-like structure composed of tightly closed fleshy scales; those of the yew which has a hard nut-like seed, in a fleshy cupule. The old gardeners also called them 'balsams' on account of another property possessed by many conifers and one which is still sometimes used as a guide to identity—the presence of sticky resin in buds, stems or foliage. This is also fallible, for other plants contain resin and indeed, not all conifers have resin.

The first book in which conifers were described in some detail was *De Arboribus Coniferi*, written in Latin by the sixteenth-century naturalist Pierre Belon. When describing conifers, Belon had our common plants in mind and almost all of which are both cone-bearing and resinous in one way or another. These trees grew in his native France or nearby countries and were for many years the only 'conifers'. Botanists have since added many others, which as plants, have major points in common. A typical wild conifer is characterised by its regular branch system and single trunk with the tree growing naturally into an upright, pyramidal form. As maturity approaches, many species lose their lower branches leaving vigorous growth only at the top of the tree. In some trees, their style of growing is more bushy, with several stems or trunks springing from the base. They vary in stature from the completely prostrate *Juniperus procumbens* to the stately Coast redwood *(Sequoia sempervirens)*, which attains 100m + in Oregon, and holds the world record for the tallest tree. Another conifer closely related to that is *Sequoiadendron giganteum*, which is most probably the largest (and oldest) living organism ever to inhabit this planet. The commercial value of the wood produced by conifers or softwoods (a misnomer, since many have extremely hard timber) is enormous. Large quantities are used annually in the building and furniture trades and also in the paper-making industry. (Just think, this page may have originally been part of a great Douglas fir growing in the Canadian Rocky Mountains.) The resin derived from conifers, when converted into turpentine by distillation, was formerly a vital part in the manufacture of paint and varnish. Although now largely replaced with synthetics, it still has its uses in some kinds of varnish and also medicine.

Garden conifers

Although different facts about the group may be fascinating, this book is primarily concerned with garden conifers which were originally developed from the wild species. Chapter 1 commences with the way in which they are classified in relation to other plants, and gives some of their origins. The second chapter deals with garden uses. Part of the advice passed on here was developed from an idea originally gleaned from Papworth's *Ornamental Gardening* published in London in 1823. In this book the landscaper is urged (and the same applies to someone gardening on a smaller scale) to think of the garden site as a bare canvas before the artist has gone to work on it. When completed, correct planting is the key to success in any garden, the canvas becoming more like a finished picture as the plants mature. Remember to construct features and plant so that there is always something to attract the eye whichever the season, be it high summer or mid-winter. Although almost every garden site is different with respect to soil, aspect and size, conifers come in such variety and form that permanent year-round interest is not difficult to provide. Having decided where to grow conifers, the next step is to discover how to grow them—our next topic for discussion. Here we find that poor soil is no problem and where it is chalky there are many which thrive. We always advocate thorough preparation of the soil; this is most important where conifers are to grow, for they have to remain in their one position for a very long time. Foresters seem so casual in their approach to this, yet seedlings planted by these experts seldom perish, but grow into fine forest trees with the (apparent) minimum of attention. Watching foresters at work, their method is to lift a spit of soil at one corner, take a small plant from a bag slung over the shoulder, drop it into the cut made, and finish the operation with a stamp from a heavy boot. Generally speaking, garden conifers require more care than this! For one thing, they are almost always larger than forest seedlings, and as they cost considerably more, the risk of financial loss is greater if they die. Regarding cost, when purchased from a nursery, good quality garden conifers can be expensive in terms of initial cash outlay. This should not deter anyone, for money spent is small when one considers the many years of pleasure they will give. When it comes to the purchase of plants of any kind, wise shoppers are wary of cheap offers, for it is invariably a case of getting-what-you-pay-for, many so-called bargains often end in disappointment. On the subject of costs it is also worth remembering that specimens take many seasons of skilled supervision before the nurseryman judges them fit for sale.

Our chapter on propagation deals with raising young plants from cuttings, layering, grafting and seed all methods in current use in the nursery trade around the world. This is the era of do-it-yourself in both home and garden so why should it not extend to producing additional plants at home? Once an initial stock has been purchased there is no reason why a keen gardener should not be able to increase many of these for further plantings. Few plants are entirely free from pests and disease, conifers being no exception to this. Fortunately for us, the garden forms appear less prone to attack than old worn out trees sometimes seen. All the same it will pay to keep a wary eye open for the signs which spell out trouble and be prepared to deal with it straight away.

Colour plates

Did not someone once say 'One picture tells more than a thousand words'? That being so, if we exchange words for the colour pictures, then this book would be very long indeed, for there are over one hundred plates! The quotation (or mis-quotation) is perfectly true of course. Seeing a picture of a living plant, often together with its natural surrounds, conveys a far more clear impression of its appearance, and sometimes uses too, than the written word. We have endeavoured to secure examples of specimens in wide variety, of various ages, growing in different places, so that the planter can get a better indication of the likely results from the plants he selects. As in our previous volumes*, to take the photographs we have used Nikon F2 cameras fitted with a variety of lenses: 35 mm wide angle, 55 mm macro and normal, and 135 mm long focus. Although these three different focal lengths were used, virtually all the shots finally selected were taken with the versatile 55 mm Micro-Nikkor which works as well in high definition close-ups as when set at infinity. A tiny Braun electronic flash gun has proved handy for some pictures taken against the light or for close-ups in dull weather. A slight enhancing of the silver in some of the pictures is due to the flash being employed to light the shadows. Plate 17 is one of these—but not those of the colourful 'blue' spruces, which were done in natural daylight conditions. We started by using Kodak Kodachrome 11 reversal film, then switched to the newer K25 from the same manufacturer. Both of the colour films give the natural rendition so important where plant photography is involved. To complete the gear carried around, we have a large white card to reflect light on to the 'dark' side of a dwarf specimen, and because of the printers' need for really sharp pictures, a sturdy tripod. Ours consists of several tubes, one fitted inside the other, when fully extended it reaches a height of over 3 m. It is said to be lightweight; we dare not think what it would be like to have to carry a heavyweight version around!

Descriptions

The descriptive list is composed of conifers in cultivation and actually offered for sale *at the time of writing*. To find out which these were, we acquired nurserymen's catalogues from twenty-seven firms in ten different countries where conifers are grown. Most of the plants offered have gone into the list, with the exception of some extremely rare kinds listed by specialists; even some of those included

* *Heathers in Colour* Blandford Press Ltd., 1974.
  Fuchsias in Colour Blandford Press Ltd., 1975.

are in very short supply. The conifers are listed alphabetically under families, genera, species and cultivars. This rather unusual arrangement is designed to show the relationship between the plants rather than follow the natural order. To find any plant required use the cross-reference index on p. 209.

1 THE CONIFERS AND THEIR NAMES

Although the differences between the various plant groups have been discerned for perhaps two thousand years or more, even the greatest botanists struggled to find the key to the correct method of their classification. Today, however, all plant life is grouped according to the natural system developed by Engler (1892) and others who demonstrated that the plants' method of reproduction as well as other characteristics must be considered together. The flowering plants comprise but one of the thirteen great Divisions of the vegetable kingdom. This in turn contains two Sub-divisions.

1 Angiospermae—in which the seeds are enclosed. Here we find grasses and the 'true' flowering plants, shrubs and trees.
2 Gymnospermae—in which the seeds are carried exposed on the scales of the female inflorescence. The latter group is the one which interests us here for within its relatively few members is found the Class of Coniferae— the conifers.

Conifer flowers are tiny and are borne in mostly short catkin-like strobili, the male and female carried separately; in most genera they are on different pedicels on the same branch—in which case they are termed monoecious. On the other hand, dioecious have the two sexes on separate individuals. Examples of these are: gingko, Chile pine and yew. The gymnosperms, or naked seed plants, differ from the other flowering plants in that the unfertilised seeds are carried exposed on the female flower instead of being enclosed in an ovary or seed vessel. After fertilisation by wind-carried pollen, the scales on which the typical cone-bearing conifer seeds are carried become tightly shut within the cone until they are mature or longer. This can take from six months to one, two, or more years according to species. When ripe, the cones open in dry weather in order that the winged seeds can drift away on the wind (*Pinus*). Alternatively, the cones break up completely with seeds and scales falling together, leaving only the central 'fir candle' on the tree (*Abies*). In the yew, the 'berries' get eaten by birds—by which means the indigestible hard kernels get carried off to sprout elsewhere. Conifer foliage is small, more often evergreen than deciduous. It can be needle and scale-like, as in the pines and spruces, or as in cypress and thuja, with flattened angular leaves which overlap clasping the stem. The leathery leaves of *Araucaria* remain on the tree for ten years or more, yew and spruce leaves last for about five, while those of the pines can be anything from three to fifteen years old before they drop. Swamp cypress is one of the few deciduous conifers and each autumn loses both foliage and the small side-branchlets on which it was produced. The leaves of a conifer when raised from seed are at first unlike those of an adult tree, the plant passing through various stages before mature foliage is seen. After germination, the seed leaves which can number from two to fifteen according to species, gives way to juvenile foliage. Finally, the normal or adult leaves appear. Some species retain an intermediate stage in which both kinds are carried at the same time. Certain specimens remain entirely juvenile.

Plant names and the binomial system of Linnaeus

The early botanists had names for plants which could consist of one or several words—really a short description. This was cumbersome, to say the least, and general acceptance of a name sometimes depended on the personal stature of its author as much as anything else. It is to the eminent Swedish naturalist, Carl von Linné, more familiarly known as Linnaeus, that we are indebted to the binomial form of naming that we use today. Although not the first to use two words for a plant's name, he established this as standard practice *for the reasoning behind it*. So authoritative was his work to become that prior to the year 1753, the date of the publication of the first edition of his *Species Plantarum*, no name given to a plant is valid today unless it had been taken up by him for inclusion in the work, or by another author at a later date. Latin has always been the international language of natural science and is still used for descriptions of new species in botanical publications. As well as for species, Latin is also used for generic names and other divisions in the vegetable kingdom.

Latin names of conifers and other plants

The scientific Latin name for the Scots pine is *Pinus sylvestris*. A closer look at the two words will tell us something of how the taxonomy, or correct botanical style, for an individual plant is arrived at. The name used as an example is that of a 'species': these are generally accepted to be a group of individuals, usually growing with others of the same appearance, whose progeny when raised from seed are virtually identical to their parent and bearing the same specific characters for generation after generation. In addition to this, species often fall into a larger group termed a 'genus', its members, although bearing a marked resemblance to one another, differ in some points. The next step up in the botanical arrangement is the plant 'family'. This consists of 'genera' (plural of genus) loosely banded together, but which again have similarities distinct enough to separate them from other such family groups. Back to *Pinus sylvestris* again: the generic name *Pinus* can be considered to belong to all the pines in general; *sylvestris* attached to a single species. In other words, there are many pines, but of these only one species called *Pinus sylvestris* in the binomial system we use.

Who can name a species?

Supposing that someone in Japan wishes to describe a plant new to science, or a Russian botanist after much study decides that a species was originally placed in the incorrect genus; what do they do so that other workers throughout the world can be kept informed of their progress? In order to get the co-operation of all nationalities for a standard system of naming, the International Code of Botanical Nomenclature has evolved. Simple in theory (although not always in practice), an agreed set of rules always applies. One, known as the 'Rule of Priority', decrees that the earliest known combination of names is valid until such times that part of the name is subsequently altered as a result of further study.

In order to secure such a name the author, as he is termed, has to describe (in Latin) in a dated, recognised botanical publication the species he considers new to science, or as happened in the past, show that he knows the details of and whereabouts of the original description or type specimen of the plant under review. Few new plants are found today, but often, as our hypothetical Russian taxonomist decides, a species was originally put in the wrong genus. When this has occurred one of two things can take place: the specific name can be linked to an existing genus, or if the plant is really distinct, it can be used to start a genus of its own sometimes taking others similar with it. Remember what we said earlier about a plant's specific name always remaining with it? Unless it results in a duplication of names, this does not change and goes with the species whichever genus it finds itself in.

Names are not changed lightly, much research is undertaken before proposals of this sort are put forward and accepted by other botanists; and when it applies to the plants we grow in our gardens the name must also be accepted by the nurserymen, and finally gardeners themselves. So the quick answer to the question of who can name a species is—anyone, providing that they keep to the established rules, although in practice it is the working botanists who undertake this sort of thing. In the case of conifers there are many synonyms which have come about as a result of changes. There are several instances of a name being used for some time before the discovery that it is antedated by another and as the earliest name is the only valid name, the existing one has to be changed. Gardeners do not always take kindly to the revised title and so for this very reason, obsolete names sometimes still appear in nursery lists. In books these names are often shown alongside the present name, together with the letters 'syn' to show that it was in former use.

Subspecies, varieties and forms

Although the species is the base on which botanical classification is founded, this is not the end of it. Certain plants do not fall neatly into the category in the simple sense of the word. When we spoke earlier of the species, we could have said that the progeny of each species is apparently identical to its parents. This is normally so, but as each seedling is a separate entity which comes about as a result of the union of the two sexes, minor genetic changes can and do occur from time to time to cause a member to differ, perhaps very slightly, from its fellows. In most cases these changes are not noticeable, but once a change has taken place, after the passage of time, the altered plant may breed to produce a group much like itself. Sometimes more vigour is the result of the ability to withstand lower temperature. This may well have happened (after a great length of time), where a species is distributed over wide range and a separate sub-species or geographical variant has taken the place of the 'type', as the original described form is termed. When growing together with the type, they are capable of freely interbreeding and of producing intermediates called 'interspecific hybrids', bearing features of both parents. Taxonomists formerly equated 'variety' or 'var.'—from the Latin *varietas*—with subspecies. Today the word 'subspecies' covers the distinct geographical races, and var. is used for a deviation from the type, individuals of which can occur mixed with it over much of its range. Although obviously belonging to the same species, these can have a distinct appearance where they are seen growing together. More difficult to classify when dealing with conifers is the word 'form', this is also adapted from the Latin. *Forma* is used to describe a wild plant found growing with the type and in which some kind of change is apparent. Perhaps they will be low growing when an upright configuration is usual; some have glaucous leaves when green is typical. When brought into cultivation both vars and *forma* of the botanists can become the cultivars of the horticulturists. The word 'cultivar' is a recent term which is described later.

Hybrids

Another class of plants comes about when two genetically close species produce hybrid offspring after cross pollinating. Although rare, these interspecific hybrids are known in the wild and in cultivation. Another kind of hybrid comes about as the result of a cross between parents in different genera. These intergeneric hybrids are extremely rare although the descendants of one of them are common. Hybrids between *Cupressus macrocarpa* and *Chamaecyparis nootka-tensis* known as × *Cupressocyparis leylandii* come into this group. Each seedling is a separate clone which means that they can be perpetuated as a line of identical plants when propagated vegetatively. From the horticultural point of view, they are especially valued, for in combining traits from each parent, their usefulness is extended.

In this case one parent provided quick growth and tolerance of dry conditions—the other contributed thick foliage, hardiness and a preference for heavy soil, all adding up to one of the finest hedging and screening subjects that we have.

Garden conifers

A garden conifer can be either a species, a subspecies, a *varietas* or *forma* or even a hybrid. The majority are, however, cultivars. Often written as 'cv' (or 'cvs' in the plural) this handy word is an abbreviated form of '*Culti*vated *Var*iety' and is reserved for 'an assemblage of plants selected for some distinctive characteristic and remaining stable in cultivation'. They can be derived from wild plants—some are, but many more have originated in nurseries and gardens. Of those found several have appeared as mutants—genetically altered in form: some tiny when tall is normal (*Picea abies* 'Little Gem'), spreading instead of upright (*Sequoia sempervirens* 'Prostrata'), or with weeping branches in place of vertical (*Taxus baccata* 'Repandens'). Occasionally a stem bears foliage with cream or yellow variegation, together with the usual green. Once propagated by cuttings or grafting (in the case of conifers never from seed) they can retain their aberration to become useful subjects for the garden (*Juniperus chinensis* 'Variegata'). Seedlings differing from the type in habit or colour or seedlings from existing cvs frequently appear in seedbeds, so these too are a source of new plant material (*Chamaecyparis lawsoniana* 'Gnome').

Cultivar names

Briefly, horticulturists accept the botanical classification of the species adding to it the cultivar name. For an example we will look at *Thuja occidentalis* 'Rheingold'. As noted previously the Latin binominal printed in italics is the species to which the plant belongs. The cv name 'Rheingold' is always printed in Roman type, commences with a capital initial and is contained in single quotes. Since 1959 a cultivar name must be a 'fancy' one, i.e. not in Latin form. The advantage of printing in this manner is that the distinction is made clear at first glance. Who coins the names for new garden plants? As long as they consider the plant worthy enough, anyone can name a new garden plant after propagating it, but in so doing must choose a language other than Latin (which is reserved for species and their descriptions). Often in English, these names can be in any tongue capable of being printed in Roman type. As with the naming of species, there is a code of nomenclature which must be adhered to. Latin was much in vogue for the often descriptive 'fancy' names of conifers prior to the introduction of the code on 1 January 1954. These such as: *alpinus, nana, pygmaea*, etc. when already given are still to be used but again, printed in Roman and contained within single quotes.

Clones

Clone is a word linked to cultivar, for many of the man-made garden plants are also clones. It is a word used to describe a line of identical plants derived from a single original and as such each is part of, and therefore identical, to the 'mother' whether it was a seedling, mutant branch or sporting bud.

In the few cases where a garden plant comprises of more than one clone, it is where the name covers a group of very similar plants often derived from a wild *var* such as *Cedrus atlantica glauca*, the Blue Atlas cedar.

The value of using a single procedure and the Latin language for names and descriptions is immediately apparent when one considers that plant study and horticulture is international and has been for several hundred years. When it comes to garden plants, we have no reason to thank some of the early nurserymen for, in many instances, they have left behind a legacy of pseudo-botanical names, many of which almost defy the memory. It is difficult enough for the seasoned grower, but pity a beginner when confronted with a tiny pot-plant complete with a label three times as high as itself and bearing the legend: *Chamaecyparis pisifera* 'Plumosa Aurea Compacta'!

2 CONIFERS IN THE GARDEN

The fact that most conifers are evergreen immediately puts them high on the list of desirable garden plants, for their inclusion in any planting scheme gives an air of permanence which is lacking where only deciduous subjects are chosen. Even where the main floral display is from the often more colourful annual flowers, roses and shrubs, the conifers are valued as they act as a foil or backdrop for the rest of the planting, and by so doing complete the garden scene. It has been suggested that successful gardens have the same qualities as that of a good picture, namely: colour, perspective, centre of interest and (by no means least) a good frame. Balance or scale comes into this too and it is only by the careful selection and placing of subjects that this can be achieved. The conifers described in these pages can provide, either alone or in company with other plants, all the components to create a garden 'as pretty as a picture'.

In developing this idea we will consider the main points in turn. Colour is something every garden needs. It seems there are some people who have the erroneous notion that conifers are just green things, the idea being based no doubt on recollections of old dusty specimens seen in towns and churchyards. This is bolstered by the fact that the majority of the conifers are evergreen. The word when applied to plants is because they retain their foliage for more than one season and are not necessarily *ever green*. Of course there are many that are just green for this is the predominating colour, but this is in every conceivable shade and few are dull. Most species have provided us with a glaucous grey or 'blue' form, others are yellow, gold or bronze often changing to a deeper tone in cold weather. Then there are those whose turn it is to delight us in the spring when their new growth emerges, brightly contrasting with the older foliage. Even in the green foliage plants there is often variegation where portions of the branchlets have a dappling of yellow and gold. Larger portions of the foliage are lacking in colour altogether and appear almost white in one or two sorts—call it a freak of nature if you like, but most attractive all the same.

The deciduous species have their day when, at the end of the growing season, their leaves assume bright autumn shades before they fall at the onset of winter. From green to clear yellow for the ginkgo, others change to burnished gold or rusty-red before dropping. Several, particularly the taller evergreens, have a silver reverse to portions of each small leaf which is particularly noticeable when branches sway in a breeze.

So it can be seen that colour there most definitely is, and not too difficult to provide with a careful selection of types. Many conifers also have attractive bark, although the trees have to be nearly mature before this becomes really noticeable as garden colour. Anyone fortunate enough to already own any of these splendid older specimens will know the value of most of the pines for their decorative bark. Even the British native Scots pines are welcome for the bright orange bark they possess. The Wellingtonia has reddish orange bark up to an incredible 60 cm (2 ft) thick on a mature tree.

Framing the garden

Just as no picture is really complete without its frame, one could say that neither is a garden complete without its frame. The main difference being that in the case of a new garden, the 'frame'—hedge or screen—unlike that of a painting, is often installed first in order to give protection to the young plants which are later to form the main part of the picture. The purpose of the hedge are twofold: one, which has been mentioned above, is to protect the garden from wind. The other is as a screen to give privacy; to stop passers-by from peering in and to hide unsightly buildings, etc. from those looking out. The type of conifer to select for any purpose depends on a number of points, the most important of which is the scale of the mature planting in relation to its surrounds. This is especially so when plants for a hedge are chosen. The hybrid Leyland cypress are ideal when a quick growing, dense screen is needed but an ultimate height of 3–4 m (about 12 ft) will be the minimum height to which they can be kept. For a lower, finished height, several of the cvs of *Chamaecyparis lawsoniana*, *Ch. pisifera*, *Taxus* or *Thuja* will be better. When something really tall is required to protect the garden from severe wind then other factors have to be considered. Climate, soil and space available for development all have a bearing on what is to be grown. In mild seacoast areas, the ubiquitous Monterey cypress *Cupressus macrocarpa* or one of its close fellows, are some of the best to have for they withstand salt-laden winds well and are quick in growth. Young plants are not always prepared to stand up to the worst of the elements, but when given a little protection in the form of other evergreen branches, or hessian stretched on stakes, they will quickly establish and very few will be lost from bad weather.

Several of the pines grow to form a dense natural barrier, there are species suitable for almost any soil or situation. Some pines grow well in cold areas and here too the Norway spruce is at home. The best plants are not those grown from 'Christmas trees' but selected forest seedlings with a good fibrous root system. For screening in cold, inclement places, one should also consider *Chamaecyparis nootkatensis* from Alaska and its hybrid offspring Leyland cypress. *Tsuga heterophylla*, the Western hemlock spruce, grows better when there is no lime present in the soil and as well as forming a dense, graceful screen, withstands clipping into a hedge surprisingly well. Another hedge plant for cold parts is *Thuja occidentalis*, which is hardier than its other North American ally, the Western red cedar. Except when planting a hedge, the subjects chosen for screening are better when set in several staggered rows in order that they can establish a wind-resisting barrier and give mutual protection more quickly. Plant thickly and thin as development takes place over the years.

Continental gardens

When driving through France we once saw a most attractive garden layout in which conifers played the main role. In flat country, the site was obviously very windy with little to stop the sea gales from tearing ordinary things to pieces. A mixture of a compact form of Austrian pine and various spruces surrounded the house on three sides with the fourth left more or less open to the sun. Around the outside of the screen were more dwarf pines and the clear blue of *Picea pungens* forms stood out clearly. Junipers both upright and prostrate were sited near the building to provide a change in colour and form. Here were also planted drifts of evergreen azaleas for bright spring colour, plants impossible to have unless protected from wind. In addition to protection from cold winds, conifers are also used extensively, particularly in hot climates, to shade the house and garden from the sun. There are many desirable residences in southern Spain set amidst the umbrella pines and other species for this reason. Here too are the dark spires of the fastigiate Italian cypress, *Cupressus sempervirens* 'Stricta', the colourful blue *Cupressus glabra* and another cypress *C. lusitanica* which originated in Mexico. Protection from sun, as well as garden beautification, is an important use for conifers in other warm climates as well. In Australasia, they compete with gum trees for this purpose and in California, too, many conifers, can be seen.

Rock and heather garden

One of the more interesting uses for conifers is that of their place as feature plants in a rock garden or heather bed. Suitable sorts blend very well with other planting in positions such as these. No heather garden is really complete without its selection of slow-growing conifers which are needed to break the flatness of the low mounded heathers.

For preference do not use any but upright forms with a moderate speed of growth unless elite specimens of miniatures can be obtained. *Thuja* 'Rheingold', *Chamaecyparis* 'Boulevard' and *Juniperus communis* 'Hibernica' and similar are the ones to choose. Prostrate or extremely slow types are better on the rock garden or bed of their own, planted with the heathers they are liable to get swamped. The heather garden is one of the few instances when solitary specimens look right—even when spaced well apart. Generally speaking, conifers not only look better when planted *en masse*, or at least in groups, but seem to grow better with others for company.

On the rock garden some kinds can go in singly, others in groups. To give an example of this: where space permits there are few nicer sights in a garden than a small gathering of the Noah's Ark tree *Juniperus communis* 'Compressa', each of varying height planted in a scree or pebble garden and accompanied by, perhaps, kabscia saxifrages or other choice things and tiny bulbs. The bright green cones of *Picea glauca* 'Conica', looking as prim as if they had just been clipped, will also command much attention when grouped together rather than spread out around the garden. They can be put to one side of the main rock work but at ground level so that their eventual height does not detract the eye from the main rock feature. Be most careful to see that they do not form a row when seen from different angles, for as Capability Brown the great landscape improver once rightly said, 'nature abhors a straight line'. Also refuse the temptation to place an upright grower at the topmost point of the rocks. Here may seem just the place for an 'Ellwoodii' or similar, put there to emphasise the height of the rockwork. But a more natural effect is to be gained by copying nature instead. In a similar situation in the wild, the upright growers are not found on the summit but instead are found sheltering in the valleys or beside rocks. We can create a natural effect by putting them on the level where they will furnish the foreground. For near the summit the more procumbent growers look right while the rounded shapes of the dwarf pines belong where they provide height without dominating the scene.

One of the more important aspects regarding the choice of suitable companions for the naturally dwarf conifers is to see that once developed they are all on a suitable similar scale. Tiny pots of alpine plants and young heathers planted at the same time as alpine conifers can so often give the wrong impression when first acquired. It may not be too long before blowsy 'alpines' and strong heathers overpower the little trees in a takeover bid for the ground space. Grouped together in a special bed of their own is about the best way of displaying a collection of these gems. Their varied shapes and colouring can give increasing pleasure as they slowly attain maturity. Really these are a fine investment, one of the best as far as gardening goes, for once planted, they require the minimum of upkeep and go on improving in appearance year in year out.

These are plants which can be placed fairly closely to start off and then spaced out as time goes by. Moved on regularly, most transplant with ease.

Ground cover and foundation planting

We read a lot about ground cover these days and all the advantages in reduced garden work when weeds are smothered. Providing the soil has been well prepared, with all perennial weeds removed, there are certain types of conifers which can be utilised for ground cover and an excellent job they make of it too.

Select from the prostrate growers such as *Juniperus horizontalis* cvs, *J. sabina* 'Tamariscifolia' and the low forms of *J. communis*. Then there are the rapid growing Pfitzers junipers where a little more height does not matter. Low growing yews and their allies can take the place of the junipers if the ground to be covered is in the shade. Another use for carpeters is on graves which need to go for long periods without maintenance, here only the smallest of the prostrate cvs will suffice.

Foundation planting is the term used in some countries including the United States for the shrubs that are used used to cover up and hide the foundations of new houses. Unlike Britain where a different system of building is employed, the ground floor level is at some height from the ground. Here, quick-growing, dense-bushy shrubs have to be employed to take away the bareness of the new walls. There are few finer subjects for this job than the many cvs of Juniperus 'Pfitzerana'. Left to their own devices many can get too large in time even here, fortunately they respond well to pruning, whole branches can be removed if needed. When tackling this job, lift the branches up and cut in a spot well out of sight making sure that they are no snags left jutting out to injure anyone passing by closely in the dark. Even where foundations do not require to be hidden, conifers can still play their role in furnishing the bare soil at the base of a house wall.

Very often there is a border left immediately adjacent to a building. This is frequently planted with bedding-out plants which are sometimes satisfactory and sometimes not. If this area were to be used to accommodate a selection of slow-growing conifers, not only would the need for annual replacements be done away with but, as permanent subjects, the conifers would provide year-round interest. While near the house, it should be mentioned that a matching pair of slender conifers are often used to make an imposing frame to the main entrance door. The dark green columns of the Florence Court or Irish yew *Taxus baccata* 'Fastigiata' can look splendid in this position. Sometimes two specimens of a cv of Lawson cypress are used instead. 'Fletcheri' would be a good choice for this position and would not need trimming to keep their dense conical shape. In the Netherlands we have seen *Juniperus* 'Skyrocket' planted right against a house wall, the blue-grey foliage rising spire-like to the first-floor eaves, to relieve the monotone of the yellow brick.

Do not forget that conifers grow well in tubs. These can accommodate smaller Lawsons, 'Ellwoodii' or 'Ellwood's Gold'; *Thuja* 'Rheingold' and Chamaecyparis 'Boulevard' are others which can be placed on the patio near the house to make an attractive feature.

Trough gardens are also better when displayed near the house for as well as being on hand to be admired they can get the watering needed in dry weather. They always require the addition of a conifer or two in order to create an established look. Only mini-size growers are wanted here, of course, once again the tiny *Juniperus communis* 'Compressa' is the favourite and first choice for most. *Thuja plicata* 'Rogersii' with its golden foliage tipped with orange is another little plant which tolerates the restrictions of a trough garden for many years. These two and other small growers will be a useful addition to the Alpine house, providing decoration when late summer and winter flowers are scarce. Bright blue when grown out of doors, 'Boulevard' is even better under glass and can cope with life in a large pot for many seasons.

The tiny growers take on a different personality when viewed from close at hand. The term 'living works of art' is usually reserved for bonsai, it could equally apply to these little gems. Should they at any time get too large for their position just pop them into the garden.

Conifers in landscape design

Earlier we wrote of the similarity between a well planned garden and a good picture. The parallel is now continued on the subject of overall design. The landscape painter has three areas to bear in mind when composing his picture. These are: the foreground, middle distance and background. The planter has exactly the same places to consider but with some marked differences. The artist puts down on the canvas his ideal view of the matured scene (either entirely real or part imagination) when seen from one position at a single point in time. The gardener's task is to attempt to visualise the mature planting as it will develop over the years—a very different thing. The other main difference lies in the fact that the painter puts down on canvas a single aspect. The gardener, on the other hand, has to consider vistas from several different approaches. In this respect he comes nearer the art of the sculptor who places his creation where it can be appreciated from different angles.

We have already seen how conifers can be used to form a 'frame' for the garden and at the same time protect the plants within. To use the word in a different sense provides the key to another valuable use for them—that of framing other planting. In Britain this is what is meant by 'foundation planting'. The successful planter uses vertical conifers in the foreground to frame the distant parts.

In former days, when great estates were laid out in a grand manner, the largest growing species were used with good effect although they are probably only now maturing the way the landscaper visualised them. Graceful cedars were placed on the lawn near the house, Swamp cypress by the lake and mighty Wellingtonias in the distance. Today, few people will be planting in this way although the same principles apply. Put some evergreen trees close at hand to accentuate the depth of the site with specimens placed strategically where they create a focal point and give perspective. The latter are rather like living statues and the choicest species should be selected for them.

When it comes to choosing specimens it is important to see that they will not get too large in relation to other nearby subjects. So, if a large grower is wanted try to give it an area to itself to prevent this happening. Few people today when planting for effect will be thinking of their great-grandchildren, they want to see results from the outset. Thinking along these lines we would not hesitate to plant a cedar which will give great pleasure for many years, although it will eventually outgrow its position and need to be felled. If it can be arranged that other plants can go instead, then so much the better for it is the hardest decision in the world to have to condemn one of these noble trees to the axe before it has reached its prime. Not all trees that have outgrown their place get removed for have we not all seen those favourites of the Victorian gardener, the Monkey puzzle, *Araucaria araucana*, dominating both house and garden? They seem so out of place to us especially when sited in suburban front gardens as so many thousands were. Most have now gone but for the occasional one hundred year old specimen towering above all. How surprised the planter who bore home the tiny potted seedling would be, if he could see his coveted possession now!

Background groups

For a background, conifers in scale with the rest of the garden are ideal. But do be careful to see that they do not get so large as to be dominant. The whole effect of a garden feature can be lost if the eye is carried past and out towards the boundary. By placing a small group of conifers at a suitable distance from the house this can itself form a background for a feature—heather bed or rockery. The eye is then drawn down to this and attention is focused on the centre of interest.

Once established these carefully sited specimens tend to hide other parts of the garden from view and as all is not seen at first glance adds a sense of mystery. This is an asset making the viewer want to find out 'what is around the corner'. On reaching the point from where the view was formerly obscured another and this time totally different vista, is opened up.

These then are some ideas for the picture*, it now remains for the artist to carry out the work.

* See also Kiaer, E. and Huxley, A. *Garden Planning and Planting* Blandford Press Ltd., 1976.

3 HOW TO GROW THEM

If there could be only one choice of soil in which to grow all the conifers it would be a well-drained, mildly acid, sandy loam. Fortunately, this restricted choice does not arise for conifers are, with a few exceptions, tolerant of a wide range of soil types both heavy (containing clay) and light (sandy). The shallow chalk soils which contain much free lime are the exception although there are suitable species which thrive even here. Many of the junipers seem to actually grow better when lime is present in the soil. If pines are wanted then there are *P. mugo*, *P. sylvestris* and *P. nigra* as well as others which will be satisfactory. *Taxus*, *Thuja* and its near relative *Thujopsis* are also content in a limy soil.

From this it can be seen that while the number of species is somewhat limited (several others are mentioned in the descriptive list) there is enough variation in these few to fulfil the average needs for hedging, screening, rock garden, winter-flowering heather bed and as isolated specimens. Except for the Swamp cypress *Taxodium*, no conifers are really satisfactory in a really wet soil or where water remains stagnant for long periods. *Tsuga* sp, the graceful Dawn cypress, *Metasequoia*, *Sciadopitys* most of the spruces and Silver firs thrive in a *free-draining* damp soil. Where there is high rainfall as well as damp soil Sitka spruce, *Picea sitchensis*, is the foresters' choice and gardeners too should find this plant of value where a quick grower is needed.

From wet places we now turn to the other extreme—that of dry, sandy soil. Almost all the pines will flourish here and as well there are the junipers and cypress which all tolerate dry conditions well.

Improving existing soil

All soil types will benefit from the addition of plenty of humus. This can be in the form of peat, compost, *old* manure, leaf-mould or debris from the forest floor. All these materials help to condition the soil, making it more amenable for planting. Where damp conditions prevail, the soil becomes more open, allowing it to dry out better; if it is of a dry nature then the humus has the opposite effect, that of retaining soil moisture. All conifers love a humus-rich soil but not too much feeding with artificial fertilisers.

Coarse sand will be a help when worked into the surface if the problem is a water-retaining soil. Where the site is wet, drainage will be the only answer for few conifers can cope with water at the roots—especially when newly planted. *Taxodium*, or as its familiar name Swamp cypress suggests, is the one conifer really at home in such conditions. Sometimes these trees can be seen with their feet actually in the water, although they will grow in normal soil too. As young plants they do not tolerate waterlogged ground as well as when they are older, so start them off on a mound of soil of sufficient height in order to ensure that the young roots are not immersed.

Conifers of all groups normally demand a light position, well away from the competition of taller trees. Where planting needs to take place in shade, select from the green forms of *Taxus* or its allies for they tolerate these places better than most. Of the junipers *Juniperus* × media 'Pfitzerana' is possibly the best to have for the shade. No coloured foliage forms of any genera are really suited to positions other than in full sunlight. Planted in shade, their brightness is soon dulled to pale green. On sun-less winter days and in a garden where light is lacking, these golden types often start reverting to green but they recover their brilliance when exposed to sunlight once again.

Hedges and screens

Preparation of the soil prior to planting should be most thorough. As permanent subjects the conifers will repay the effort over their many years of development. For a hedge, the ground should be trenched, breaking the sub-soil with a garden fork but not turning it over. Next spread some humus in the form of compost (garden variety), well-rotted manure, moist peat or leaf-mould in the base of the trench before turning in the top-spit again.

Do not confine the digging simply to the line of the proposed hedge for roots must be encouraged to spread outwards from what will become an evergreen canopy. This is almost as efficient as an umbrella in keeping the rain off the soil and because of this, the sheltered area immediately beneath the branches tends to become dust dry in many soils. A wide-spreading root system will ensure that the roots do not suffer from lack of moisture for this reason.

Spacing depends on the species chosen. A single row of Leyland cypress can be put in 1 m (about 1 yd) apart down the centre of the dug area. Many Lawson cypress, *Thuja* or *Taxus*, should be closer than this, say 0·8m (2½ ft).

When *Cupressus macrocarpa* are used to form a strong hedge they are frequently put in a double (staggered) row at 1-m centres (1 yd apart in two rows) with 0·5 m (1½ ft) between the rows. In a suitable soil they will meet up within three to four years and if need be making a barrier against the worst sea-coast storms.

Do not forget to allow for lateral spread as well as height when deciding on a line for the hedge; of course, clipping will reduce this considerably when comparing a hedge plant with one that has developed naturally. The mature hedge must also receive plenty of light if it is to remain furnished to the ground.

Plant when the soil is moist without being waterlogged. Risk of total failure occurs when young conifers have to stand in water for several weeks after planting and this can happen in some soils when the dormant season is chosen as the time for setting out. Whenever possible try to see that the soil is warm enough for new roots to form quickly; if the soil or air is dry a light overhead sprinkling with water will be much appreciated by the young plants. A little general ferti-liser worked into the soil surface, a few days prior to planting out, will provide an incentive for the roots to travel and make establish-ment just that little bit quicker. Feeding should only be attempted on a very small scale for we do not wish to encourage too much soft top growth at the expense of root formation. This is especially so for the first season or two.

For hedging purposes small plants are to be preferred to speci-mens. Quite apart from the not inconsiderable higher extra cost of established trees the smaller versions are more likely to grow away in an even manner. As young stock tends to transplant more readily, these would probably overtake the older plants in a few seasons any-way.

Individual trees, especially of such shallow rooters as Leyland cypress and *Cupressus macrocarpa*, when used for hedging should each receive the support of a stake or bamboo for the first two or three seasons. Put in at planting time and see that it is strong enough to take the weight of a wind-blown plant. Alternatively, the transplants can be tied loosely to a strong wire stretched the length of the hedge line. The movement at soil level of an unsupported youngster is a great hindrance to it taking hold. Remove the stakes or ties when it is judged that the hedge has established a secure root system.

Nipping back of growing points by taking off about a third of the current season's wood has to be done in order to encourage bushiness. The season of planting will not be too soon for this to start. There is no hurry to get the garden shears out for a while as little in the way of regular trimming is required until individuals begin to meet up. Once started, an annual trimming will be needed in mid-summer when the growth for the season is slowing and also a tidy up in the spring.

The best shape for a hedge is when the base is fairly wide with a gradual slope inward towards the top. Unlike a hedge in which the sides are perpendicular, this wedge-shape allows light to reach each plant more easily resulting in better, more even growth. Once the plants begin to meet is also the time to decide whether or not to have a hedge which will require trimming, or a screen.

For a screen, the conifers that started off as a hedge are thinned by removing every other plant leaving the remainder to grow on without trimming. Where a strong windbreak is wanted, several rows are planted with a stagger. No, this does not mean that one has to be intoxicated to tackle the job! It is simply a way of describing alternate equal spacing in the rows.

Specimens

Specimen conifers that are to be displayed in grass are planted in prepared stations of at least 1 m (1 yd) in diameter. Dig out the top spit and place to one side. Break up the sub-soil, removing rocks or stones. Spread some humus source material in the bottom of the hole then backfill to the depth of the base of the conifer. Next, place the plant in position, staking first if deemed necessary. Complete the operation by filling in around the root-ball and firming as required. Keep the prepared area free of grass or weeds for several seasons until the specimen is maturing and able to compete. In wet sites the soil can be mounded slightly to allow the surface to drain. Where the ground is likely to be really dry, a saucer-shaped depression is suggested—this tends to retain any moisture.

Mulching the ground around conifers is most beneficial, for it helps to keep the soil moist and cool; it can be decorative too. For this use a thick layer of peat, screened garden compost, leaf-mould or shredded bark. We have even seen seashells used for this purpose. Before mulching see that the soil is moist and free from weeds.

To feed or not

If anything, most conifers prefer a soil that is on the poor side rather than one rich in feeding. This is not to say that young plants do not respond or that it should be denied them. In the nursery area around Woking in England and Boskoop in the Netherlands, as well as elsewhere, there can be seen magnificent stocks of growing-on conifers of every kind in which feeding has played an important part in their development.

The soil is manured, often annually, and fertilisers added too. This is very often a fish meal or other organic compound. The aim is to establish an ideal fibrous root system which allows the plant to be lifted, transported, then replanted—often hundreds of miles away— without trouble. On poor soils, conifer roots tend to be sparse, growing long and coarse in their search for sustenance. For the garden plants a little added nutrient in the form of dried blood, hoof and horn, fish or bone meal will give a boost to growth with better foliage colour too. Just before the plants start to grow in the spring is the best time to apply feeding of this type. Just sprinkle it on the soil surface and very lightly hoe it in. Should the weather be dry at that time a gentle watering will ensure that it starts working right away. One must be more careful with the slow growing or Alpine conifers for these are easily forced out of character if feeding is overdone. For these, a mulch of moist peat or shredded bark should suffice.

The type of plant to select—planting and how to avoid losses

Purchased stock comes in a variety of ways. Some are bare-rooted from the open ground or perhaps have been grown in the soil then lifted with a root-ball that is kept intact with a piece of hessian (burlap) or polythene film. Others are pot-grown; formerly in clay pots, these days more likely to be seen in metal or polythene containers.

Hedging conifers, Lawson cypress and thuja are frequently bare-rooted. This is satisfactory provided the young plants have been lifted regularly or undercut to induce a fibrous root-system. If well rooted, there is no reason why these cheaper plants should not grow away well and develop into a fine hedge or screen. If the roots appear to be dry, soak them in a bucket of water for several minutes before planting out. The soil mark on the lower part of the stem indicates the former position in the ground of the growing plant—use it as a guide to the depth for replanting. Keep a damp sack ready to lay over the roots of plants waiting to be planted as the sun and a drying wind can cause irreparable damage if roots are left exposed. Unable to plant right away due to unsuitable soil conditions? Do not worry. The young trees can be 'laid in' in a vacant plot until you are ready to deal with them. When planting, firm with the heel if the soil is moist or dry but less pressure when wet. If really soggy, it will be better for the plants if the operation is delayed until soil conditions improve.

Bare-rooted conifers can only be put in when they are dormant. Using root-balled stock extends the planting season for a few weeks. In fact, if handled carefully, conifers lifted several months previously and kept with their roots plunged in moist peat can often be planted in mid-summer. Many materials used for wrapping roots will rot if left intact—others do not. The latter must be removed but *only after the plant is in its prepared station*. Pot-grown plants have a distinct advantage over the others that are normally sold as dormant stock, they can be purchased for planting the year round. The purchaser also benefits by being able to select when convenient, then delay planting until conditions are suitable—perhaps weeks ahead. Losses of container-grown conifers are very few indeed if the advice of soaking pots (for several hours if dry) is heeded. Allow them to drain thoroughly before planting in the prepared site. In dry weather, it is also a good plan to water the soil the previous day in order that it too can drain by the time the plants are ready to go in. If, after the container is removed, it is seen that the roots in the pot base are very matted, these can be teased out carefully with a pointed stick. Do not break the root-ball or much of the object of growing the plant in a pot in the first place will be lost.

Container grown or containerised?

Sometimes masquerading as container-*grown* are container-*ised* plants. These have been produced in the open ground then placed in a container for selling purposes. This is not to say that there is anything wrong with the plants; in fact, they can be better than some old subject that has outgrown its pot. Yet what sometimes happens is, when removing the pot, all the compost falls away leaving a bare-rooted, open-ground plant. If it is consequently treated as such (after registering a complaint with the vendor!), watered, and kept shaded, there is every possibility that transplanting will be successful. These open-ground plants if purchased after they have re-established themselves in their containers compare very favourably with stock which has been container-grown throughout its life. Some conifers, notably junipers, do not make much root when grown in pots and care must always be taken to ensure what little there is, is kept intact, when transferring from pot to soil.

Reducing losses

Most losses of recently planted stock are due to lack of water during their first season of growth. This applies to all transplants—especially evergreen and conifers. As well as maintaining a moist soil, they appreciate a gentle overhead spray now and then. Movement at root level was mentioned earlier as another cause of conifers failing to become established. This is remedied by staking the young plants. If lack of water is the chief killer of new stock, a close second is cold wind. To lessen its ravages, much good will be done by erecting a temporary screen of hessian canvas supported by stakes on the windward side. This can instead be a shelter of evergreen branches or hurdles which will assist the young conifer by reducing transpiration or water loss from the foliage caused by drying wind and/or sun. Special transplanting sprays, in which the leaves receive a coating of lacquer-like material, are much in vogue in some countries. We have not used these ourselves but feel that anything that can help a plant to get through this critical time must be considered an asset.

Selecting quality plants

What does one look for when selecting conifers from a garden centre or nursery? Whether growing in the open ground or in containers, the plants to choose are those which are young, vigorous, well-furnished stock, typical of the species or cultivar. 'Well-furnished' means that foliage should be carried well down, almost to soil level and with little trunk or stem visible.

There are some exceptions to this. In an immature cedar, for example, the stem will be seen although the other points apply. When due to being grown too closely in the rows or kept in a pot too long, thuja or Lawson cypress have lost the foliage from the lower branches this is seldom replaced. Such trees are best passed over in favour of younger stock which still carries plenty of foliage low down.

Where dwarf or slow-growing conifers are involved and there is a choice between large grafted plants and smaller specimens on their own roots, choose the latter for they will develop into plants more typical of the original form. Grafted stock will be recognised from the bump on the stem just above the soil mark. This is where the two halves of the plant have been brought together. When offered they are generally the only ones available due either to the difficulty in rooting the particular cv, or other economic reasons.

Where tall growers are concerned, the 'blue' spruces, *Picea pungens* cvs cedars and the like, any worries over speed of growth will not apply. With these, try to ensure that it is a nicely balanced plant that is selected. This should have an evenly spaced branch system, together with, in the case of an upright grower, an erect, *undamaged* leader. This latter advice also applies to those species which have been raised from seed, for where the leading bud has been damaged in early life, two or more replacement shoots appear with the result you either get an uneven specimen or a tree with two trunks.

Now a warning about really pot-bound plants. On tipping the

plant from its pot, a hard mass of tangled root is seen. Unless new roots can be coaxed from the hard ball which was once potting compost, little in the way of new growth can be expected. These plants are seldom satisfactory even when released from their pot prison.

Stock that has its origin in forestry nurseries seems to fall in two distinct categories. Young seedlings of forest conifers of two or three years old are excellent value providing they have been transplanted. Older plants on the other hand are, generally speaking, not a good 'buy' for unless undercut they have remained unmoved for many seasons and instead of having a fibrous root system theirs are coarse and stringy.

Nurseries are built on the reputation of the plants they sell. Most offer perfect quality although sometimes the choice seems rather restricted considering the range available. This applies especially to the alpine conifers. For these there are specialists who concentrate on nothing else.

4 PROPAGATION

Most conifers planted in gardens are purchased from a commercial grower, garden centre or nurseryman. Once a stock has been obtained in this way there is no reason why an enthusiast should not be able to raise more plants from many of these for additions or replacements to his collection. Propagation of trees falls into two main categories.

1 From seeds — This is termed seminal propagation and is used for species only.

2 From portions of an existing plant — This is vegetative propagation and is the way of increasing all cvs and clones of species.
   The latter category can be further subdivided into:

   a Cuttings
   b Grafting
   c Layering
   d Division

Raising conifers from seed

The dropping of ripe seeds to the forest floor is nature's way of raising replacements for the old trees. In extreme cases it needs a forest fire to heat the cones left on the tree before they open to disperse their contents. The seedlings resulting from the seeds that the forester sows in nurseries will eventually be used to plant new areas or for re-afforestation. All *species* of conifers can be raised from seed to produce a plant the carbon copy of its parent.

Although the growing of conifers from seed is practised on a vast scale by foresters and to a lesser extent by nurserymen, it is seldom attempted by gardeners. The reason for this is clear from the sentence above, for apart from a few species, almost all the garden conifers are cultivars which do not breed true from seeds even if they were available. Anyone wishing to grow species and able to obtain seed will find it about the easiest way of propagation. Seed may be sown as it ripens, or sowing can be delayed until weather conditions are suitable. The site chosen for a seed-bed should be in a sheltered position and should be a light sandy-loam for preference. Shading from the hot sun must be provided or the tiny seedlings, which would normally have the shelter of their parent, will wither and die. The plastic netting now available is suggested for use on a small scale or other materials such as hurdles made from birch branches can be used instead. Seeds are sown either in drills or broadcast in narrow beds. After covering with soil or sharp sand the surface can be firmed with a light roller. Patting down with the back of a spade will suffice in a small bed. The firming is done to prevent the top few centimetres from drying out and therefore assists the germination process. The actual depth of sowing depends on the size of the individual seeds but it is never more than a light covering. To ensure sturdy growth thin spacing of the seed is important. Pests will be discouraged if, before sowing, the seeds are shaken in a polythene bag with a little powdered red lead oxide and sufficient paraffin (kerosene) to dampen them. If this is not done, mice and other rodents will dig them up in their search for food. Moles can also be classed as pests with their burrowing and earthworks. Mothballs placed in their runs are said to drive the moles away, but trapping or gassing may have to be resorted to if the mothballs prove ineffective.

The shading described above is needed after the seeds are sown and before the tiny plants appear above the surface. Fix the material right over the width of the narrow bed so that no part gets the direct rays of the sun. Transplanting to a sheltered nursery takes place after at least a full season's growing.

Seeds in pots

For most gardeners, the alternative to sowing in the open is to place small quantities of seed in pots. An open-textured compost is required, this can be made up from three parts of moist peat, two parts screened loam and one part clean sharp sand. No fertiliser will be needed at this stage but a dusting of ground chalk can be added for junipers and yews. Precautions must be taken to ensure that earthworms do not enter through the drainage hole in the base. Worms cause damage to tiny roots that are forming. It was possible at one time to use small circles of perforated zinc, which when slipped into the bottom of the pot did the job admirably; plastic mesh now seems to have taken the place of zinc. After providing some sort of drainage the pots are almost filled with the prepared compost, then watered and stood to drain through for an hour or so. Next the seeds are sprinkled thinly on the surface of the compost and lightly covered with a layer of sharp sand or very fine grit, labelled and placed in a frame or greenhouse for germination.

Seeds germinate better when the pots are darkened with thick brown paper; this is removed as they break the surface. As in the open beds, frames must also be shaded in sunny weather. When growing satisfactorily, the pots should be placed on a gravel base in a sheltered spot out of doors. Potting off is carried out when the plantlets are large enough to handle, sometimes before the true leaves are showing. They can be grown-on in pots until ready for their permanent places or put in a nusery bed for a few seasons. Remember to transplant young plants every two years to ensure a fibrous root system. When grown-on in pots, they need a little feeding if the same compost as used for seed raising is used. A small amount of general fertiliser can be incorporated in the mix—or liquid manure can be put in occasionally with the watering.

Some are grafted

Forms or mutants, of which garden plants are mainly comprised, do not however come true from seed. These have to be propagated vegetatively by one or more of the four methods mentioned at the beginning of this chapter. This means that the variation which occurred in the original plant is physically carried over to the next generation, and all the descendants are therefore part of the original. In many instances, including most of the pine cvs, cuttings are very difficult or impossible to root under normal conditions. These cuttings or slips (scions) have to be grafted-in to a rooted plant, usually a seedling, of the same or a related species. Once a union has taken place, the top growth of the stock is removed entirely to allow the scion to develop as a new individual. Nearly all conifers can be induced to form roots, some with comparative ease, others are more difficult. Generally speaking grafting should only be undertaken in the latter case. Sometimes this is not found to be so in this commercial world of ours. A comparatively 'easy rooter', but slow grower, will be found to be a grafted plant when purchased. The quick production of an even stock is demanded of the modern nurseryman. Once he has produced a saleable sized plant, apart from the cheaper price, from the planter's point of view there is nothing initially to choose from between a grafted conifer and one on its own roots. It is where the dwarf or slow-growing plants are involved that there can be cause for concern. Here, the more vigorous rootstock usually exerts an undue influence over the rate of growth, causing too much top to develop just when small size was the aim. So in this case, whenever possible, go for a plant on its own roots.

How conifers are grafted

Grafting, especially of ornamental subjects, has always been regarded as the height of the propagator's skill. In many establishments it is still done behind the locked doors of the 'prop house', with only the keyholder knowing of the successes or otherwise of his efforts! Yet, on paper at least, it looks easy enough, just a matter of having the right materials at the correct time, a sharp knife and a little simple carpentry.

If it really were that easy, the *mystique* which surrounds the operation would have long been swept away. In practice, especially where conifers are concerned, much experimenting will need to be done before any degree of proficiency can be claimed. This is not to say that first-class grafted plants are beyond the scope of the amateur enthusiast, for they have been and still are being produced.

Although it has been proved possible to carry out the grafting of this group in the open, because of lack of control over the elements—drying wind, excessive rain, etc.—it is better to tackle the operation under glass. Almost all grafting takes place on to seedling stocks of the same species which have been established in pots (for at least a season) beforehand. An exception to this is in nurseries when often due to the large numbers involved, young Lawson cypress are lifted just prior to 'working'—which is then done on the bench. These so-called 'bench grafts' are then placed thickly in a propagating frame for the union to take place. We know of a nursery where this is regarded as a job for wet weather and one which gives the men a welcome chance to sit in a warm shed listening to sport on the radio, while carrying out their delicate task.

The time for grafting conifers

The two usual times for grafting under glass are early spring, just when the sap is rising in the stems of 'brought-on' stocks, or late summer when growth has firmed. Unless one is using dormant stocks, it is the latter season which is suggested for the pines. Their resinous sap flows freely in the spring and on exposure this hardens and prevents an efficient join from taking place.

Of all the forms employed, side-grafting is the most frequently used for conifers. In this, a slice of wood is removed from the stock as low down the trunk as possible. The lower the better, for this minimises an unsightly bulge in the trunk in later years. A cut is then made in the base of the scion which corresponds to that of the stock, cut surfaces are quickly brought together and secured with raffia. The top growth is left on the stock at this stage, although it can be reduced in size if over large. Once the union has taken place and the scion is showing healthy foliage or growing the stock growth above the join is removed altogether. A thin cane is sometimes needed at this stage to support the two halves of the new plant in case they part company before they are firmly united as one.

Under glass there is no need to protect the wound against the weather as there would be outside; in fact by providing a trap for moisture it could be detrimental to the plants' health. Loosen the tie as the join swells, for the material used could cut into the bark and by so doing lessen the flow of sap to the scion. Successful graftings will have to be hardened off before lining out in a nursery row or re-potted as the case may be.

Grafting *versus* cuttings

Many conifers that can only be purchased as grafted plants will be found to be perfectly satisfactory when grown on their own roots. *Chamaecyparis obtusa* cvs are almost always seen as worked or grafted plants in nurseries. These will grow roots themselves quite success-fully, although growth is slow—and is congested in the dwarf forms. This makes cutting wood difficult to find, as one normally looks for shoots of the current year to use for propagating. In the case of these and other tight growers, it often proves too short to handle easily. When this happens it is in order to try wood that is two, three or more years old. Some conifers, including a good many of the junipers and in particular the juvenile foliage forms of *Chamaecyparis*, are very easy to root. Others are not too easy. The introduction of plant root-ing hormones in a powder or liquid base has enabled the keen plants-man to have a better chance with some of these. Where no special misting equipment is available, most conifers can be rooted in pots placed in a lightly shaded frame during the summer months. 'Double glazing' with a sheet of thin polythene stretched under the light will do much good by increasing the humidity in their particular micro-climate. Almost all conifers will show a higher percentage of rooting when treated in this way, although an exception seems to be Lawson cypress which recent research has shown to do better under a single-glazed light.

It will be found that rooting takes place more quickly if the cut-tings can be prevented from wilting. This can be achieved by main-taining a relatively high air humidity rather than allowing the rooting compost to get too wet.

Filled pots of cuttings are kept under cover until growth recom-mences in the spring, when they can be lined out in the soil or potted-on as required. For the latter, a compost similar to the one suggested for seed raising can be used, plus the addition of a very small amount of general fertiliser.

Taking cuttings

To take cuttings, use a sharp knife or razor and trim to a heel or node between two seasons' growth. After dipping the base in rooting hormone, insert the prepared cuttings up to a third of their length (short cuttings can go in up to their middles) in a mixture of two parts moist sphagnum moss peat and one part clean, sharp sand. Pots or boxes can be used as containers according to the number of cuttings that are to be handled.

In practice it will be found to be easier if each cv is kept to a separate pot, as the length of time taken for rooting can vary, from three weeks to six months or longer, from the time the cuttings are inserted. When the pots are filled with cuttings, they should be watered with a fine rose water-can to settle them in. They are now taken to the mist bench or propagator in the greenhouse or placed in a shaded garden frame (it is better to site the frame in a place out of direct sunlight rather than apply shading to the glass). The pots should be kept just moist and the best way of watering is to place the pots in a bucket, allowing the water to soak up from the base. After rooting, a little more air is admitted to the frame and in winter the lights may be left slightly open except in frosty weather.

Time for taking cuttings

In our early working days on the nursery, the traditional time for taking cuttings was always late summer to autumn. Since the widespread use of soil-warmed, mist-irrigated benches in glasshouses has come into being this time has changed, for cuttings are now put in every day of the year. There are some species and cvs that seem to have their time-for-rooting preferences (experts call this their 'optimum time') and once discovered success is assured.

Choose the correct propagating material

The correct selection of wood for cuttings or grafting is important where conifers are concerned, for unlike many plants that have the ability to form a typical specimen no matter where the wood originated, many are unable to do this. Instead they continue to grow in a similar manner as if they were still joined to the tree, even after propagation. Thus, scions from downward-sweeping branches of some species tend to produce procumbent growers. Only leading or apical shoots from the top of the plant have the ability to form a balanced tree with a normal radially opposed branch system—and these have to be selected to produce the best-shaped trees. Because of the scarcity of suitable shoots that can be used for grafting purposes, nurserymen use lower parts complete with an apical bud. With correct training these can make a tree hardly differing in shape from

43

one developed from a leader. The Silver firs, *Abies* sp and the spruces, especially *Picea pungens* (glauca group) are the ones to take especial care with. There is a high demand for the latter, so they are frequently sold as one-year grafts and come complete with a thin cane. This has to be replaced as the plant grows, making sure that it continues to develop in an upright manner until the lower branches are well formed. Any plants produced at home will also require staking and great care must be taken with the topmost bud, for if damaged, the plant will not grow in a shapely manner.

On a rock garden, the procumbent growers belonging to this group sometimes throw a leader. When this happens, peg the strong growth down or remove it altogether in order to retain the plant's original form.

Basal growth of some cvs often retains the juvenile character of the original cutting when used for propagating material. *Thuja* 'Rheingold' is one of these. It makes a rounded, fluffy ball of old gold foliage (instead of becoming conical in form) if shoots are selected from well down in the plant instead of from the leading shoots bearing adult foliage. These small plants have often to be maintained artificially by removing the adult foliage as it forms.

All conifers which develop in an atypical way due to the selection of propagating material have been termed 'cultivarients' by Mr H. J. Welch in *Dwarf Conifers*, his standard work on the subject. Although not yet accepted by the naming authority, the word accurately conveys how many of these forms come about.

Cuttings from vigorous young plants, especially seedlings, usually root more readily than material taken from mature trees. Some nurserymen keep their mother plants growing soft, under glass, to maintain a constant supply of quick rooting material. The gardener who simply wants just a few extra plants need not go to these lengths and may well find the answer on page 46.

Layering and division will very often provide a good alternative method for increasing stock to rooting cuttings or grafting, especially where low growing plants are involved. The two methods are discussed here together as they have basic similarities. In each method, roots are induced to form by placing lower branches beneath the soil. Division entails lifting a plant then replanting at a greater depth with only the tips of the branches showing above soil level. The latter is only really suited to low growers and alpine conifers. Once rooted (soil can be scraped away to check on progress) the plant is dug up, carefully divided and the rooted pieces lined out in a nursery row. Layering *in situ* entails less work. Here the selected portion is pegged down in some good compost for roots to form.

On plants that are shy rooters, the roots can be induced to form by wounding the bark. To do this, carefully make a diagonal slit in the base of stem and apply a rooting hormone powder to the cut. Layers put down at any time of the year have the advantage that they can remain in position without disturbing the mother plant for two or three seasons before being finally cut away. Rooting progress can be checked by partially exposing the branch and when it appears to be well rooted, severed from the parent. Do not transplant the layer for several weeks during which time it will make much more root fending for itself, if moved beforehand it could resent the disturbance and die.

An old-fashioned nursery

Since the advent of the modern mist propagation technique and its twin advantages of the speed and ease with which roots can be put on cuttings, division of conifers is seldom, if ever, employed in commercial establishments any more. At one time, there was a small select nursery in the Woking area of Surrey, England where the owner produced by this method some of the finest dwarf conifers and heathers that we have seen anywhere. The stock plants of *Chamaecyparis lawsoniana* 'Ellwoodii', *C. pisifera* 'Plumosa Compressa' and 'Nana', *C. thyoides* 'Ericoides' dwarf yews, *Cryptomeria japonica* 'Vilminiana' and several others were selected, lifted, then replanted deeply. This was done in the autumn. Twelve months later, they were again lifted and this time divided up, graded into various sizes and replanted. Another full growing season then elapsed before the larger plants of the stock were ready for sale. This was also the time to take out the mother plants from these to once again be planted and repeat the cycle. As this was taking place on several plots each year, it ensured a regular supply of top quality plants. The greensand soil in those parts, when provided with plenty of peat and laced with manure, produces conifers that lift with a good root-ball and develop a foliage colour which is never to be forgotten.

As a postscript to the section on propagation there is one final method which is handy for someone wishing to increase his stock by one or two plants. On most dwarf conifers some of the lower stems will be found to have self-layered. These 'Irishman's cuttings' with their few roots can be detached and lined out for a season or two until well-rooted enough for them to be planted up permanently.

5 TROUBLES

The problems that affect the correct development, damage or even death of conifers are varied; some are avoidable from the outset, others can be corrected. Of those avoidable, the most common cause of failure is in transplanting; the so-called physiological disorders often come into this category too. They are largely overcome by the correct selection and placing of species to suit the soil and climate. A smaller loss comes about through fungus attack; insect pests have also to be countered for they are not only responsible for the spread of some fungi but can themselves cause disfigurement.

Transplanting

Although the subject has been dealt with in Chapter 3, transplanting and the two or three seasons it takes for the plant to re-establish accounts for a possible 99% of actual losses or partial failure. The most common problem here is water, either not enough or too much of it. Newly transplanted, the conifers are at their greatest risk from drying winds and hot sun. In exposed places, steps should be taken to prevent water-loss through evaporation. Placing a temporary shelter made from hessian or plastic screening material around them will largely overcome the problem. If weather conditions permit, a fine spray of water can be given overhead in the evening.

On the other hand, too much water can be as bad or even worse than not enough. We have been called in to advise on a thuja hedge, newly planted in wet, sticky clay soil which was a virtual failure. Holes were simply dug in the soil which filled with water after the plants went in and the roots literally drowned through lack of air. If the planter had mounded the soil very slightly along the line of the hedge they would most probably have survived and done well.

Physiological disorders

Selecting the correct plants to suit the soil, climate and position will largely eliminate symptoms of physical disorders that may appear. It is obvious that losses of tender subjects will occur if they are planted in a climate that is too harsh for them. A late frost can also nip the shoots of a normally hardy form. If this happens after the new tips are showing these can shrivel and brown; sometimes new buds take a whole twelve months to develop from the leaders, with the result that no growth is made for the season. Trees usually make a good recovery when they grow away the following spring.

Chlorosis, yellowing of the foliage in a green plant, is most often the result of planting a calcifuge or lime-hating species in a soil containing an excess of lime. This comes back to correct selection again, for there are many which dislike alkaline (limy) soils. Saying this does not help anyone already owning a sickly plant because of this. What to do about it? Transplanting to a new position prepared with lime-free compost may be the answer where a dwarf plant is involved. Alternatively, an iron chelate such as Sequestrene can be watered in around the plant according to the maker's instructions. This will provide iron in a form that is readily taken up by the plant which should soon turn a healthy green again. Unfortunately, this is not a permanent cure and doses will have to be repeated at least twice each year.

Another cause of chlorosis is the too liberal application of fertiliser or fresh manure near the roots. Conifers do not, as a rule, show symptoms of other soil deficiencies.

Leaf scorch

Caused by wind, sun or frost, leaf scorch due to the lack of chlorophyll in the leaves is common especially on the white or yellow variegated forms. These have to be planted in the sun for their special feature to develop, so try to place these in a spot sheltered from wind where they get the early morning sun but remain out of its direct rays by midday.

Foliage scorch can also come about by splashing or contact with wood preservatives or their fumes—be careful when treating a wooden fence if there is a hedge close by. Wind-blown weedkillers—

especially the selective type—will also cause damage to tender growths. Once again, care must be taken to avoid this happening. Chemical sprays when used for pest control do not appear to harm conifers. If there is a choice, use wettable powder formulations avoiding any that are oil-based as the latter obscure the 'bloom' on the foliage and once covered this takes many months to reappear.

Diseases

Diseases of conifers are caused through fungal infection. Fungi are primitive forms of plant life often living in the soil and in or on plants. Many of these are beneficial to other plant life, some conifers have a partial symbiotic relationship with a fungus in which the two rely on each other for their existence. Although many species of conifers (sometimes whole families) appear to be completely immune from disease, others are frequently victims of attack. In all cases, plants kept in good growth by attention to their cultural needs are less liable to succumb.

There are a great many diseases and symptoms vary. These include: discoloration or dropping of needles and leaves, rust-like patches on foliage and dead or dying branches. In most instances it is only practicable to treat young or dwarf trees. Spraying with a fungicide in spring and late summer (two applications at each time) will clear up minor attacks of most diseases. Others are more severe and will entail cutting away infected branches, which should then be burned. The wounds left must also be treated using an antiseptic paint. It is as well to use a sterilant on any cutting tools used to lessen the risk of spreading infection.

Where a tree has died as a result of disease and not just old age or drought, it too must be burned and the ground planted with a non-woody plant for four to five years before replacing a conifer in the same spot.

Insects

Some conifers are attacked by several insect pests which have to be killed before they cause unsightly damage to the plant and, by weakening it, allow the spread of fungal diseases. Spray with an insecticide two or three times at two-week intervals during the early spring and again in late summer—or at any other time the pests are spotted. As with diseases, it is the young plants which need this special attention in order for them to maintain their vigour.

As well as spraying against normal pests, galls which appear as swellings on the shoots of Norway spruce can be picked off by hand. These are colonies of tiny aphis which, if left, will stunt the tree. Caterpillars defoliating pine shoots can also be picked off where they can be reached, or a spray used for these too.

We have recently come across a combined aerosol pack which contains a fungicide and insecticide together. Although expensive this appears to be really effective, clearing up an attack of red spider mite on a specimen *Picea abies* 'Gregoryana' very quickly.

6 GROWTH RATE AND ULTIMATE SIZE

It is probably true to say that for many, the ideal conifer would be one which quickly attained its desired size and shape and then maintained this more or less indefinitely without further growth. Woody plants such as conifers are not like animals (which grow until they mature then remain the same size), but instead they continue developing until such time that their life span is ending. Then growth finally ceases and a decline begins. Even many of the small 'alpine' sorts can become large in time, unless regular pruning, undercutting or transplanting is done. Where hedging and, more particularly, screening plants are concerned, we want the opposite; quick growth is the main reason for selecting certain kinds for this purpose.

In addition to the individual characteristics of each species or cv selected, there are other factors which govern the growth rate and affect the ultimate size of most conifers. These are:

1 Soil
2 Situation
3 Climate

The latter can be easily seen where the same kind of plant is growing in different countries with varying climates. Under perfect conditions for the species, speed of growth and eventual height is frequently as much as double that of where the plants are growing in less suitable places. Because of the variability experienced, we do not always mention expected sizes in the text. For those wanting a rough guide the following notes may help.

Rock garden conifers

Where plants are suggested for rock or heather garden use most of these should not exceed 2 m (6 ft 6 in) in height or spread after ten years growth.

Specimens small and large

Moderate growers selected as isolated specimens can be expected to reach some 2–4 m (6 ft 6 in–13 ft) after a similar length of time, although this will depend largely on the size of the original specimen at planting time. The ultimately very tall trees normally commence

Some typical conifer

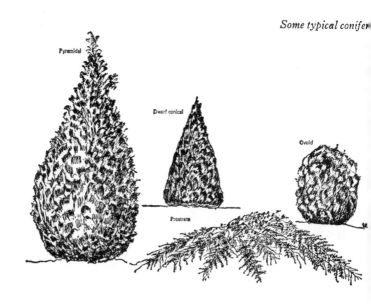

Pyramidal

Dwarf conical

Ovoid

Prostrate

life with a burst of speed, slow down then, filling out over the years.

Hedges and screens

Planted in reasonable conditions, most of the plants mentioned will be well on the way to fulfilling their purpose after five years of growth.

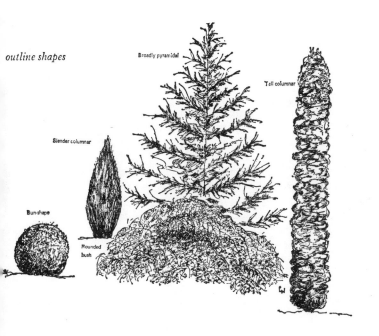

outline shapes

Broadly pyramidal

Tall columnar

Slender columnar

Bun-shape

Rounded bush

Minimum winter temperature zones

Workers at the Arnold Arboretum, Jamaica Plain, Mass., USA, devised a system of hardiness zones for North America based on likely or average lowest winter temperatures. These zones are numbered from 1—10 and are also a useful guide to the relative hardiness of conifers in other parts of the world.

The purpose of including the zone numbers in the Descriptions is to convey a rough indication only: borderline plants placed in exposed positions may succumb in extreme weather—others, where it is more sheltered, could come through unharmed. Other factors are involved in this too; dry or moist air or if the plants have a protective cover of snow. Most of Britain comes into Zone 8. This means that all plants rated at Zone 8 or lower should survive once they are established.

	°C	°F
ZONE 1	—45	below —50
ZONE 2	—45 to —37	—50 to —35
ZONE 3	—37 to —28	—35 to —20
ZONE 4	—28 to —23	—20 to —10
ZONE 5	—23 to —20	—13 to —5
ZONE 6	—20 to —15	—5 to 5
ZONE 7	—15 to —12	5 to 10
ZONE 8	—12 to —6	10 to 20
ZONE 9	—6 to —1	20 to 30
ZONE 10	—1 to +4	30 to 40

THE COLOUR PLATES

1 *Torreya nucifera*

2 *Taxus baccata* 'Semperaurea'

3 *T. bacc.* 'Dovastonii Aurea'

4   *Agathis australis*

5   *Araucaria heterophylla*

6 *Chamaecyparis lawsoniana* 'Fraseri'

7 *Ch.laws*. 'Hillieri'

8   *Ch.laws.* 'Gnome'   9   *Ch.laws.* 'Minima Aurea'

10   *Ch.laws* 'Gimbornii'

11   *Ch.laws*. 'Westermanii'

12 *Ch.laws.* 'Lutea'

13 *Ch.laws.* 'Forsteckensis'

14 *Ch.laws.* 'Pygmaea Argentea'

CHAMAECYPARIS
LAWSONIANA
'PYGMAEA
ARGENTEA'

15 *Ch.laws.* 'Fletcheri'

16 *Ch.laws.* 'Filiformis Compacta'

17 *Ch.laws.* 'Chilworth Silver'   18 *Ch.laws.* 'Ellwood's Gold'

19 *Ch.laws.* 'Snow Flurry'

20 *Ch.laws.* 'Duncanii'

21 *Ch.laws*. 'Albovariegata'   22 *Ch.laws*. 'Green Globe'

23 *Ch.obtusa* 'Kosteri'   24 *Ch.ob*. 'Nana Lutea'

25   *Ch.pisifera* 'Filifera'

26 *Ch.pis.* 'Filifera Aurea'

27 *Ch.pis.* 'Filifera Compacta'

28 *Ch.pis.* 'Compacta'

29   *Ch.pis.* 'Gold Spangle' (*front*); *C,pis.* 'Boulevard' (*rear*).

30   *Ch.pis*. 'Plumosa Aurea Compacta'

31 *Ch.pis.* 'Boulevard'

32   *Ch.pis.* 'Squarrosa'

33 *Ch.pis.* 'Squarrosa Intermedia'

34 *Ch.pis.* 'Plumosa Compressa'

35   *Ch.pis*. 'Snow'

36   *Ch.obtusa* 'Tetragona Aurea'

37   *Thuja occidentalis* 'Ericoides'

38   *Ch.pis*. 'Squarrosa Sulphurea'

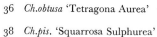

39 *Ch.obtusa* 'Fernspray Gold'

40 *Cupressus glabra* 'Variegata'   41 *C.gl.* 'Pyramidalis'

42   *C.macrocarpa* 'Goldcrest'

43   *C.sempervirens* 'Swane's Golden'

44   *C.mac.* 'Horizontalis Aurea'

45 *x Cupressocyparis leylandii*

46 *Thuja occidentalis* 'Lutescens'

47 *Th.plicata* 'Old Gold'

48 *Th.occ*. 'Caespitosa'

49 *Th.orientalis* 'Conspicua'

50 *Th.or*. 'Beverleyensis'

51   *Th.or.* 'Juniperoides'

52   *Th.or.* 'Aurea Nana'

53   *Th.occ.* 'Rheingold'

54   *Th.or.* 'Rosedalis'

55   *Juniperus communis* 'Compressa'   56   *J.squamata* 'Blue Star'

57   *J.procumbens*

58   *J.proc.* 'Nana'   59   *J.chinensis* 'Obelisk'

60   *J.sabina* 'Tamariscifolia'

61　*J.communis* 'Hibernica'

62 *J.com.* 'Depressa Aurea'

63 *J.virginiana* 'Grey Owl'

64 *J. x media* 'Hetzii'

65 *J.chinensis* 'Pyramidalis'

66   *J.recurva var coxii*

67 *J. x media* 'Pfitzerana Aurea'

68 *Cedrus deodara* 'Aurea Pendula'   69 *A.lasiocarpa* 'Compacta'

70 *A.balsamea* 'Hudsonia'

71 *A.pinsapo* 'Glauca'

72 *A.procera* 'Glauca'

73 *A.concolor* 'Glauca Prostrate'

74 *Cedrus deodara*

75 *Picea brewerana*

76 *P.abies* 'Ohlendorffii'

77 *P.abies* 'Little Gem'

78 *P.pungens* 'Globosa'

79   *P.mariana* 'Nana'

80   *P.abies* 'Nidiformis'

81 *P.glauca* 'Conica'

82　*P.abies* 'Echiniformis'

83　*P.pungens* 'Glauca Prostrate'

84   *P.omorika*

85 *P.orientalis* 'Aurea'

86 *P.mariana* 'Doumetii'

87 *Pinus parviflora* 'Glauca'

88 **P.cembrioides** 'Globe'

89　*P.nigra* (rear); *P.mugo* var *pumilio*

90 *P.mugo* 'Gnome'

91 *P.leucodermis* 'Compact Gem'

92 *P.sylverstis* 'Argentea Compacta'

93   *P.densiflora* 'Pumila'

94   *P.mugo* 'Mops'

95   *P.montezumae*

96 *P.nigra* 'Hornibrookiana'

97 *P.sylvestris* 'Pumila'   98 *P.syl.* 'Aurea'

99   *Pseudotsuga menziesii* 'Fletcheri'

100   Cone of *P.muricata*

101   *P.mugo* seedling

102 *Sciadopitys verticillata*

103 *Tsuga mertensiana* 'Argentea'

104　*Larix kaempferi* treated as a bonsai

105　*Tsuga canadensis* 'Pendula'

106 *T.can.* 'Bennett'

107 *T.can.* 'Jeddeloh'

108 *Sequoia sempervirens* 'Prostrata'

109 *S.semp.* 'Adpressa'

110 *Dacrydium cupressinum*

111 *Cryptomeria japonica* 'Cristata'   112 *C.jap* 'Sekkan-sugi'

113 *Podocarpus acutifolius*

114 *Podocarpus totara* 'Aurea'

115   *Cryptomeria japonica*

116   *C.jap.* 'Compressa'

117   *C.jap.* 'Globosa'

118   *C.jap.* 'Bandai-sugi'

DESCRIPTIONS

GINKGOACEAE   Ginkgo family

Ginkgo

A remarkable race of primeval plants of which but a single living species remains. Eventually growing from 15–30 m (50–100 ft) in height, this is a hardy deciduous tree with unusual, un-conifer like foliage. *Ginkgo* is not only of great botanical interest but also a highly decorative ornamental which thrives in a variety of soils, and being tolerant of atmospheric pollution is suitable for city gardens. Growth is upright, generally pyramidal, its undivided, fan-like, leathery leaves are green when in growth but change to clear yellow before they drop in the autumn. The sexes are on separate trees, under ideal conditions the females bear crops of round green fruits which ripen yellow emitting a peculiar odour when they fall. New plants of the type are grown from seed sown under glass in the spring; cvs have to be grafted using the seed-raised plants as stocks.

Ginkgo biloba   Maidenhair tree or Ginkgo tree   ZONE 4

The single species from China, where it has long been cultivated and no longer appears to be a wild plant.

— — 'Autumn Gold'
Male clone with regular conical outline which was selected for the splendid autumn coloration of the foliage.

— — 'Fastigiata'
With its branches held almost erect this is a narrowly upright form.

— — 'Fairmount'
This male plant is of distinctly pyramidal shape.

— — 'Pendula'
A rare sort with weeping branches.

— — 'Tremonia'
A conical plant which originated in Germany, where the *ginkgobaum* is a popular, hardy tree.

TAXACEAE   Yew family

Taxus

The yews are a small group of evergreen conifers with decorative foliage well-known for their ability to flourish on most soils either chalk or acid, provided that it is well drained. Apart from the golden foliage cvs, their garden usefulness is extended by their tolerance of shady positions in beds and borders. As they are able to withstand frequent clipping, another garden use is for hedging. The linear leaves are deep, shiny green in the species and, although spirally attached to the shoots, are often arranged in two rows. Male and female flowers are normally on different trees and the cvs being clones are therefore either male or female. Male flowers are small, profuse, releasing clouds of pollen when disturbed. The females shortly after fertilisation develop into a nut-like seed which is carried on a green disc. The holder swells as the seed ripens to form a brightly coloured fleshy cup (aril). The seed is very poisonous to animals (including humans) and the foliage more or less so, for it is known to us to have killed horses yet has left sheep unharmed. The species can be increased by sowing seeds during the spring either outside or under glass. The cvs will root from firm wood cuttings placed under glass; low growers can be layered. Nurseries frequently graft choice kinds under glass during the spring.

Taxus baccata   Common yew or
English yew   ZONE 6

Growing to about 10 m (33 ft), this is a familiar small tree in the British Isles, where, as well as being one of only three native conifers, it has also been in cultivation since ancient times. The species has dark green, almost black foliage arranged in two rows on the side branches and radially on the leading shoots. A fine plant for hedging.

— — 'Adpressa'
Spreading shrub with small oval, pointed leaves, deep green above, greyish beneath. Fairly slow growing, sometimes classed as a dwarf but eventually tall.

— — 'Adpressa Variegata'
As above, but with new leaves golden and becoming gold-edged as they mature.

— — 'Amersfoort'
An unusual form with sparse branching. The dark green leaves carried densely on the short side branchlets are thick and almost round. Slow growing and suitable for the rock garden. 'Rushmore'

is a recently introduced little charmer with a similar style of foliage; it occurred with normal seedlings in Messrs Robinsons Nursery, Knockholt, Kent, England.

—— 'Aurea'   Golden yew
New leaves golden yellow becoming pale green in their second year. An upright, dense bushy plant, highly valued for hedging or as a clipped specimen.

—— 'Dovastoniana'   Westfelton yew
A large wide, spreading bush or small tree with horizontal branches with weeping side branchlets clad with dark green leaves.

—— 'Dovastonii Aurea'   Pl. 3
A cv of French origin with similar style of growth to the preceding cv, but with all the foliage yellow-margined.

—— 'Elegantissima'
A choice yellow and green variegated plant of compact habit. This is a female clone and is most effective when carrying a good crop of red berries.

—— 'Fastigiata'   Irish yew
    Florence Court yew
This is the well-known columnar form, the erect branches bearing dark green–black leaves. Old specimens become wide-topped with several leaders.

—— 'Fastigiata Aureomarginata'
    Golden Irish yew
Similar in outline to the above, but with clear yellow emerging leaves which later become yellow or gold margined.

—— 'Lutea'
An attractive female clone with yellow 'berries' nestling in the dark green foliage.

—— 'Nutans'   Dwarf yew
A tiny much-reduced compact bushlet with dark green irregularly arranged leaves. This is sometimes labelled 'Pygmaea' in nurseries, although this is a different cv with *light* green leaves.

—— 'Repandens' Spreading English yew
Wide-growing plant with green foliage. With its downswept branches, which have drooping tips, this makes an interesting lawn specimen.

—— 'Semperaurea' Pl.2 Evergold yew
Dense bushy grower with very bright gold and cream foliage retaining its colour well throughout the seasons.

—— 'Standishii'
This is a choice, very slow grower which develops into a compact column of brilliant golden foliage.

—— 'Washingtonii'
An open-branched shrub of very wide growth. Leaves are pale yellow, rather long, curving upwards on the semi-weeping branchlets.

T. cuspidata   Japanese yew
   ZONE 4

A tree of moderate size in its natural habitat, but almost always only a shrubby bush in gardens. Slow growing and hardy, it differs from the more common English yew by its longer winter buds. The rather leathery leaves have a yellow reverse. Many cvs have been named in North America, where it is generally more hardy than the Common yew.

— — 'Nana'
Dense and wide growing, this plant has thick branches with short shoots and radially arranged, dark green leaves.

T × *media*   Anglo–Japanese yew
   ZONE 5

Hybrids between *T. baccata* and *T. cuspidata*, more or less intermediate between their parents. Hardier than the English yew, the various clones offer a range of hedging plants, specimens and even low ground cover. More than twenty have been named, the three mentioned below are the most frequently listed.

— — 'Hatfieldii'   Hatfield yew
Named after Mr Hatfield who first made the cross, this is a compact grower with lustrous dark green foliage.

— — 'Hicksii'   Hicks yew
This has naturally conical growth and is a good selection for hedging purposes.

— — 'Thayerae'   Thayer yew
Fast growing, vase-shaped form with long branches of shining green foliage.

Cephalotaxus

A genus of evergreen shrubs or small trees, the species of which are found wild in Asia. Closely resembling the yews and formerly included with *Taxus*, at least one authority has even taken *Cephalotaxus* out of the Taxacae to form a family on its own. The main difference between the Plumyews and *Taxus* is in their large acorn-like fruits; *Torreya*, another cousin, has spine-tipped leaves. Plumyews tolerate shady conditions well and, like the yews, prefer chalky soil. When available, seeds grow readily; cvs are increased by cuttings placed under glass in late summer, preferably with a little bottom heat. Layering *in situ* will be possible in many cases.

C. fortunei   Chinese plumyew
   ZONE 7

A large, upright, bushy shrub or small tree with attractive long glossy green leaves and large oval fruits.

C. harringtonia Japanese plumyew   ZONE 5

Similar in habit to the above. Both
are frequently seen as leaderless
bushes, this has smaller leaves,
pale green in colour.

—— var *drupacea*
One of the more commonly seen
forms of these interesting plants,
this has light green sickle-shaped

leaves. 'Prostrata' is a spreading
clone of the *var* which is useful to
cover a shady spot in any soil.

—— 'Fastigiata'
Recalling the upright Irish yew in
form, this also has the same
strictly ascending growth the
branches bearing clusters of large,
dark green leaves. Slow growing
although eventually tall this is one
of the hardiest of the group.

Torreya

Yew-like trees generally regarded as being more of botanical interest
than garden subjects. This is not to say that a mature specimen with
its red bark, almost black foliage and semi-pendulous branch system
does not have a pleasing appearance. The linear foliage is really very
dark green, yellowish beneath, rather stiff, terminating in a hard
point which is spiny in the Californian nutmeg tree. The individual
leaves spring out radially from the shoot; in side branchlets they
appear to be in two opposite rows. In most species the leaves are
strongly scented. The two sexes are usually on separate bushes; the
small yellow male flowers often conspicuous in the leaf axils. The
female develops into an ovoid olive-like fruit with a fleshy covering
to the wrinkled seed. Like the yew and its relatives this genus also
contains plants which are shade tolerant and indifferent to limy soil.
Seeds offer the best method of increasing one's stock, they can be
sown in pans, under glass, during the spring. Cuttings will also root,
these should be inserted in sandy compost also under glass but in
late summer.

Torreya californica Californian
nutmeg   ZONE 7

A tree to 30 m (95 ft) in its native
habitat but in cooler parts of the
world (such as Britain) normally
a large shrub or small, broadly

pyramidal tree. The spreading
branches and pendulous shoots
are clad with long, glossy green,
yew-like leaves. The nutmeg in
the name refers to the large thick-
shelled, nut-like seed.

T. nucifera Pl. 1 Japanese Torreya ZONE 5

This tall tree from Japan, like its
American cousin, is usually seen
as a large bush away from its
homeland. Of rather thinner appearance than the foregoing it
also has smaller leaves. This is
dark green, carried in opposite
rows on the shoots, curving and
ending in a hard point. The seeds,
rich in oil, are said to be eaten by
the Japanese.

ARAUCARIACEAE Chile pine family

Agathis

The Kauri pines, close relatives of the Monkey-puzzle tree, are
natives of several countries of the Pacific, including Australia, Fiji,
Malaysia and New Zealand. They are noted for their heavy, tall,
straight trunks which are often devoid of lower branches on mature
specimens. The bark is thick and exudes a latex-like fluid when
wounded. The separate flowers of each sex are found on the same
tree. Cones are round, breaking up when ripe to release seeds and
scales together. The evergreen foliage is large, flat and leathery and
persists on the tree for many years. Propagation is from seeds sown,
when ripe, under glass.

A. australis Pl. 4 Kauri ZONE
9

A noble tree endemic to New
Zealand and which was formerly
of considerable economic importance for its high quality timber.
Away from their native rain forest
they do not attain such great size
and therefore make attractive specimens for park or garden
planting, a growth rate of some
5 m (17 ft) in ten years can be
expected in suitable warm areas.
They are not hardy in Britain.
The foliage is thick, lime-green in
colour, and up to 8 cm long and
1 cm wide on a young plant. As
the tree matures the leaves get
shorter and darker in colour.

Araucaria

These imposing trees are only found growing as wild plants in the
southern hemisphere and all but one—the familiar Monkey-puzzle—
are tender. Their growth is symmetrical with branches carried to the
ground when young; older plants usually lose their lower branches

as they age, developing into an upright tree with a well-rounded crown. The flowers of each sex are usually borne on different trees. The fertile cone breaking up when mature can be very large and contains edible seeds in most species. These seeds offer the most reliable means of increase although cuttings of terminal shoots can be tried in a heated propagator. The latter method is used to propagate *A. heterophylla* in Europe.

A. araucana syn *A. imbricata* Monkey-puzzle or Chile pine
ZONE 7

This tall, hardy tree with its stout trunk, long sweeping branches complete with dark green spine-tipped leaves is almost too familiar to need a detailed description. Planted extensively in Britain in a former era, its popularity is now on the decline in favour of smaller growing subjects. Quick growing but slightly tender when immature, the best specimens are to be seen in country areas well away from city or industrial smoke.

A. bidwillii ZONE 10

Found in the wild in the coastal area of Queensland, Australia, where it is called Bunya–Bunya by the native aboriginals, this is ultimately a tall tree with a pyramidal outline. Young plants have a particularly neat manner of growth, as they mature much of

their foliage is shed and in the long lower branches only at the ends will hang the bunches of shining bright green, sharply pointed leaves. Although not hardy in Britain, we have seen these interesting trees planted in warm Mediterranean gardens.

A. heterophylla Pl. 5 syn *A. excelsa* Norfolk Island pine
ZONE 10

Under ideal conditions a tall tree with a straight trunk and almost horizontal branches. These bear two types of foliage: soft awl-shaped on juvenile shoots and hard sharply pointed deep green leaves on mature and cone-bearing Branches. Frost tender, the cv 'Gracilis' with its bright green *Cryptomeria*-like juvenile foliage is often sold as a tub or pot plant in many countries for indoor decoration (outdoor in warm weather).

CUPRESSACEAE   Cypress family

Austrocedrus

This genus comprises of a single most attractive species of small tree which as its common name (below) suggests is a native of Chile. Formerly included with *Libocedrus* and sometimes still listed as such, it differs from these in foliage detail. Until examined closely it could be taken for that of *Thuja*, another relative. Male and fertile flowers are on the same tree. New plants raised from seed, cuttings could be tried.

Austrocedrus chilensis Chile cedar   ZONE 7

This seldom seen species forms a handsome, columnar spire. The scale-like leaves are pale green in colour and marked with grey stomatic bands beneath. It is carried in flattened sprays, finely divided towards the ends.

Callitris

The Cypress pines are of value for their ability to cope well with arid conditions. As can be expected, these tall shrubs from Australia are only suited for cool greenhouse decoration or the mildest of sea-coast localities in Europe. In warm climates they are attractive trees for garden use. The stems or branches are long, thread-like, clad with tiny green leaves. Both sexes of flower appear on the same tree, coning begins early. Stock increase is from seeds or cuttings grown in sandy compost under glass where the atmosphere should be kept close until growth has started.

C. columellaris Murray River pine   ZONE 8

An erect growing large shrub or tree most often seen with several trunks. The thread-like shoots with their scale leaves give a greyish sheen to the tightly packed branches. This makes a superb specimen tree for very hot, dry areas.

C. oblonga Tasmanian cypress pine   ZONE 8

Usually grown as a shrub, hedge or tub plant this species like the foregoing also carries grey foliage composed of scale-like leaves on thin shoots arranged in clusters. The seeds are found in round, almost black, cones and offer a ready means of increasing stock.

C. rhomboidea Oyster Bay pine
ZONE 9

Of the thirteen known species of Cypress pines, only three are likely to be met with in cultivation and this plant is the least common of the three. The thin branchlets are clothed with typical scale-like leaves which vary from blue-grey to sea green. A subject for the mildest areas only.

Calocedrus syn *Heyderia*

Formerly included with *Libocedrus*, this small genus of evergreens is also related to *Thuja*; all three have a similar general appearance. In *Calocedrus* the young leaves are fairly long then become more scale-like and carried thickly on the shoots in opposite pairs; they are free at their pointed ends. Branchlets are flattened, held in fan-shaped sprays. Flowers of the two sexes appear on the same tree with their small cones ripening at the end of their first year. Young stock can be raised either from seed or cuttings, cvs are from cuttings only. A closed frame can be used for propagation and protecting immature plants.

C. decurrens Incense cedar
ZONE 5

Apart from the two cvs which follow most, if not all of the plants in cultivation are of the form 'Columnaris' or 'Fastigiata'. These develop into tall, very narrowly columnar trees of un-mistakable appearance. With shining green leaves and reddish stems and trunk these make splendid lawn specimens when either sited singly or in groups. The wild plants found in the South-Western United States usually have a looser, more open way of growing.

—— 'Aureovariegata'
An attractive slow-growing plant with large, irregular patches of light yellow foliage interspersed with the usual green.

—— 'Intricata'
Of American origin, this seedling is a dwarf form which is unlikely to exceed 1 m (3 ft) in ten or more years. Growth is upright, foliage intricate with a golden bronze hue to the young leaves.

C. formosana ZONE 9

More open in growth than the hardy species this plant has light green leaves and a white trunk. It occurs in thin forest of deciduous trees in Taiwan (Formosa), specimens have survived in similar situations in southern England.

C. macrolepis ZONE 9

Another choice half-hardy species suited to mild parts only. Its lightgreen leaves are held in the characteristic flat, fan-like sprays.

Chamaecyparis

Formerly linked with *Cupressus* and often erroneously still listed as such, this important group of evergreen trees, which although consisting of a few species only, has provided us with many favourite garden conifers. In most of the species the typical young plant is conical in outline, before filling out to become bell-shaped. In others, the foliage is not retained to ground level, so that one or several trunks will be formed. Seedlings commence life with soft, awl-like leaves before assuming their familiar flat branches, which are composed of tiny stem-clasping scale leaves. Male and female flowers appear on the same tree and except for *C. nootkatensis* (which takes two years), most of the others ripen their cones in the first year. Species are increased by sowing seed in a prepared site in early spring, cvs need to be propagated by vegetative means: cuttings in a cold frame during autumn—'difficult' sorts can be grafted under glass during the spring using seed raised Lawson cypress as understocks. Providing that they have been shifted regularly all the members of this group transplant readily—even when quite large specimens. The many cvs exhibit the greatest variation from the wild plants both in colour of foliage and form.

Ch. formosensis Formosan cypress ZONE 6

The giant of the group with a height of over 70 m (230 ft) recorded in its native Taiwan where they grow in the alpine zone from 2000–3000 m. It has attractive foliage which is rather rough to the touch, resembling *Ch. pisifera* in form, bright green with bronze tints in the autumn and white beneath. Young trees are subject to frost injury but gain hardiness with age. In spite of its eventual large size, the plant is slow growing in cooler climates.

Ch. lawsoniana Lawson cypress ZONE 5

A valuable timber tree of up to 60 m (190 ft) in North America and increasingly used for forestry in Britain. The type forms a tall stately specimen of green or greyish foliage, pyramidal or columnar in habit with the leading shoots drooping at the tips. Since the introduction of seeds from Oregon and California to Lawsons Nursery, Edinburgh, Scotland in 1854, the flow of numerous variants has been unending. They come in all shades: green, yellow, silver, blue and sometimes variegated, some tall, others dwarf. Because of the vast range of colours and shapes this tough group has become one of the most popular groups of conifers in Britain and Europe. Although not very tolerant of salt-laden winds, inland they are completely hardy. The best specimens of all are those planted in a moist soil in a cool climate.

— — 'Albospica'
Of conical form and slow growing this has green foliage tipped with white variegation.

— — 'Albovariegata'   Pl. 21
Ovoid in shape and often treated as a dwarf although in time it can attain 3 m (10 ft) .The dark green foliage is liberally interspersed with white shoots.

— — 'Allumii'
An old cv with grey-blue leaves which is still widely planted. The branches are at first compact and upright but later becoming more open as the tree gets tall.

— — 'Aurea Densa'
A tiny dwarf pyramid of soft, bright golden foliage which was raised at Messrs Rogers & Sons former Red Lodge Nursery, Southampton, England.

— — 'Aureovariegata'
Robust pyramidal tree with much creamy-white variegation spread through the normal green foliage.

— — 'Blom'
A slower growing form of 'Allu-

mii' from which it was a sport. It has similar upright growth but brighter 'blue' leaves.

— — 'Columnaris' syn 'Columnaris Glauca'
A superb plant which forms a narrow spire of bright blue foliage. Fine where space is restricted.

— — 'Duncanii'   Pl. 20
This plant with fine grey-green foliage on thread-like stems was raised in the New Plymouth, New Zealand nursery of Messrs Duncan & Davis. It forms a rounded bush of compact growth.

— — 'Ellwoodii'
A well-known little conifer with grey-green juvenile foliage which makes a fine choice as an upright subject for the rock garden, tub or lawn specimen. Although slow growing, they can get surprisingly tall in time unless trimmed lightly each year. There are also several mutations in cultivation with the same dense, upright form. 'Chilworth Silver' (Pl. 17) or 'Nyewoods' is light silver-grey; 'Ellwood's Gold' (Pl. 18) raised at Hilliers Nursery, West Moors, Dorset has pale silvery green foliage overlaid with gold becoming brighter in winter, this needs a sunny spot to show good colour; 'Ellwood's White' on the other hand is inclined to burn if planted in full sun for its white patches of foliage displayed against the normal green are almost devoid of chlorophyll; 'Ellwood's Pygmy' forms a round

bun, cut out reversions on this; 'Fleckellwood', recently introduced in New Zealand, is upright and has creamy-white or yellow patches.

— — 'Erecta Viridis' syn 'Erecta' Bright green foliage in erect, flattened sprays. Dense growth when young, later becomes more open, usually with several leaders. Because of the particularly clean appearance of the young plants, this is a popular clone in spite of the fact they will require tying up in future years to prevent snow damage.

— — 'Erecta Filiformis' syn
 'Mason's Erecta'
Upright growth with thin thread-like stems of bright green. Ought to be more planted than it is!

— — 'Erecta Aurea'
Of similar foliage arrangement to 'Erecta Viridis' but with bright golden leaves. Slow growing, eventually forming a flat-topped bush, perhaps 1 m tall after many years. Rather prone to damage from bad weather.

— — 'Erecta Alba'
Robust grower which makes a neat pyramid. Uncommon, it has white tips to all the branchlet ends.

— — 'Filiformis'
Thin appearance when young with sparse branches, but later building up into a broad-based pyramid of narrow, grey-green thread-like shoots. Older plants can be tall with the shoots hanging in drooping clusters. 'Filiformis Compacta' (Pl. 16) is a dwarf plant which forms a mound of similar foliage. 'Filiformis Glauca' has thin 'blue' stems, large in time it makes a plant as wide as high. All of these plants are generally more uncommon than the thread-leaf forms of the Sawara cypress which are described on page 141.

— — 'Fletcheri' Pl. 15
A popular conifer of only moderate growth rate and ultimate size. Although the semi-juvenile blue-green foliage can be damaged by harsh winds, this is seldom noticed in normal garden situations where the plant forms a dense pyramidal column usually with several leaders. 'Fletcher's White' is slower growing kind well marked with creamy-white shoots. 'Snow Flurry' (Pl. 19) raised in New Zealand also has much of the normal foliage replaced with cream patches, a vigorous grower. 'Yellow Transparent', another mutation, has feathery, clear yellow leaves. 'Gold Splash' has large patches of gold well displayed against the usual silver-grey

— — 'Forsteckensis' Pl. 13
A tight ball of dense, light green foliage which can be retained in its dwarf state by annual removal of shoots which protrude above the surface.

— — 'Fraseri' Pl. 6
A clone resembling 'Allumii' with

dull grey leaves which is very common in cultivation. It is hardy, reliable, forming a pyramidal shape with its fan-like branches held almost vertically at first.

— — 'Gimbornii' Pl. 10
Almost globular, this has dark green foliage marked with mauve at the tips. Slow growing it is a fine plant for the rock garden or a tub.

— — 'Gnome' Pl. 8
A variable plant developed by Mr Don Hatch at his former Heath End Nursery, Farnham, Surrey, England. In its best form it is one of the slowest growing of all the Lawsons making a ball of bright green foliage. May grow to 30 cm (12 in) after twelve years. 'Green Globe' (Pl. 22) is very similar, it arose independently in Messrs Palmers Nursery, Glen Eden, Auckland, New Zealand.

— — 'Golden King'
This unmistakable golden conifer was raised in Holland. The tree is of moderate size with a rounded top, columnar or pyramidal in outline. The large drooping sprays of pale yellow foliage tend to bronze in cold weather.

— — 'Grayswood Pillar'
An extremely narrow pencil-like column of blue-green foliage arranged in vertical branchlets.

— — 'Green Hedger'
Dense upright grower with bright green foliage. This was a seedling selected by Messrs Jackmans Nursery, Woking, Surrey, England for its value as a hedging plant.

— — 'Green Pillar'
A light green pyramidal tree of only moderate growth rate, which although the branches are strictly ascending, these do not suffer from snow damage as might be expected.

— — 'Hillieri' Pl. 7
Possibly the best of all golden Lawsons, this has light yellow, feathery sprays on a tree of moderate size.

— — 'Imbricata Pendula'
This New Zealand raised clone has the most unusual, yet graceful appearance of the group. The pale green whipcord type of foliage hangs down in very long strings to form an elegant weeping tree.

— — 'Intertexta'
A large tree of elegant form with regularly spaced, drooping branches. The foliage is dark green with a glaucous bloom. An old cv in cultivation for over 100 years.

— — 'Kilmacurragh'
Raised in Ireland this is probably the finest of the erect, columnar group. Unlike 'Erecta Viridis', the bright green ascending branchlets suffer little damage from a fall of wet snow.

— — 'Knowefieldensis'
This very slow grower forms a

flat-topped mound of dark green, rather hard foliage.

— — 'Kooy'
An upright, glaucous blue tree of moderate growth with a regular conical outline.

— — 'Lane'   syn 'Lanei'
A superb light golden yellow foliage plant, upright it forms a perfect specimen or luxurious hedge.

— — 'Lutea'   Pl. 12
The clear yellow foliage of this old cv, which is still commonly planted, is carried in feathery sprays. The tree eventually makes a broad-based column.

— — 'Lycopodioides'
A strange plant with thin, grey, cylindrical branchlets, often twisted and curled. This can grow into a large bush almost triangular in outline.

— — 'Minima'
A slow grower with densely-packed, upright fan-like sprays of slightly glaucous green foliage. Of value as a rock plant or for container growing.

— — 'Minima Aurea'   Pl. 9
This gem is virtually a clear yellow version of the above. Slow growing, it is the favourite small golden conifer for the rock garden.

— — 'Minima Glauca'
This dense growing round bush very slowly attains about 1 m (3 ft 3 in). The upright and side-ways growing fan-like sprays of deep green rather glaucous foliage radiate from the short trunk.

— — 'Nana'   syn 'Nana Glauca'
Possibly the most widely planted of the 'Minima' group. Once mature, this can be recognised by the taller central trunk and pointed top. Under good growing conditions the foliage develops a fine glaucous sheen.

— — 'Nidiformis'
A round leader-less bush with a central depression bearing some resemblance to a huge green birds' nest. Eventually too large for a small space.

— — 'Pembury Blue'
This splendid recent introduction has leaves of the lightest silver-blue. Of moderate size; it grows into an upright tree, more open and pyramidal than its Dutch-raised rival, 'Columnaris'.

— — 'Pottenii'
With soft, light green, semi-juvenile foliage, this forms a cigar-shaped column. Good growing conditions and a clear area around the tree are essential to prevent the base from becoming shabby.

— — 'Pygmaea Argentea'   Pl. 14
syn 'Backhouse Silver'
A small growing round bun with dark green foliage edged in silver. A choice miniature raised by Messrs James Backhouse, York, England at the end of the 19th century.

—— 'Rogersii' syn 'Nana Rogersii'

Fine green-blue foliage on a slow growing, rounded plant but retaining a perfect shape only when trimmed. Left alone the bush tends to form a leader of coarse foliage.

—— 'Silver Queen'

This broad-based pyramid has large, spreading branchlets of pale green leaves heavily overlaid with white. Particularly attractive when making creamy-white new growth in early summer. Several similar in colour have been raised, including 'Limelight' and 'Moonlight'.

—— 'Smithii'

Although only a loose bush when young, this golden Lawson develops into a dense upright column.

—— 'Spek' syn 'Spek's Glauca'

Raised in the nursery of Jan Spek, Boskoop, Netherlands this plant has steel-blue glaucous leaves carried on a robust tree, upright, pyramidal in shape.

—— 'Stewartii'

An elegant, hardy tree conical in form its yellow branches shading to green at the base. Popular the world over it was raised at the Ferndown, Dorset nursery of Messrs Daniel Stewart & Sons.

—— 'Tamariscifolia'

This rounded leader-less shrub of deep green spreading branches is often confused with 'Nidiformis'

because of its similar shape. This makes an interesting specimen either in a collection or as a feature plant.

—— 'Tharandtensis Caesia'

Given time to develop this round bush-like conifer can get too large for the rock garden for which it is often selected. The foliage is deep glaucous blue with the sprays compressed and thick.

—— 'Triomf van Boskoop'

Frequently planted, this glaucous clone ultimately makes a large open tree, columnar in shape. Old specimens invariably lose their lower branches.

—— 'Versicolor'

This broad-based, upright grower has green leaves banded with yellow which from a distance suggest that the whole plant is pale gold.

—— 'Westermanii' Pl. 11

Another wide, pyramidal form. This has large, heavy sprays of yellow foliage with golden weeping tips. Although tall eventually, it is of moderate growth rate making a splendid isolated specimen.

—— 'Winston Churchill'

Slow-growing upright tree of classic pyramidal shape, but sometimes with a rounded crown this has foliage of the richest yellow. We have often admired the originals in Messrs Hoggers Nursery, Felsted, Surrey, England where it was a seedling introduction in 1945.

—— 'Wisselii'
An upright tree of vigorous growth which can be confused with no other. The greyish trunk bears sparse branches clad with dark green fern-like clusters of leaves.

—— 'Youngii'
A pyramidal tree, eventually tall, the dark green foliage is carried in frond-like sprays.

Ch. nootkatensis   Nootka cypress or Yellow cypress   ZONE 4

In the wild, old trees of this species are very tall with large trunks devoid of branches for several metres from the bole. In cultivation, they are usually seen as slender pyramids only filling out with age. The branches are spreading, green foliage slightly rough to the touch, the branchlets which are held upright when young later become semi-pendulous with their tips drooping. They are very hardy and make good garden plants where a quick growing, ultimately tall tree is desired. In general, the Nootka cypress is not too fussy about soil although their preference is for a moist rather than dry position. The cones which take two years to ripen are round with four to six scales protecting two or four seeds under each. Seeds can be used for raising young plants, but

all the cvs are normally grafted using *Thuja orientalis* as under-stocks.

—— 'Compacta'
A very slow-growing sort which makes a loose bush of light green foliage.

—— 'Glauca'
This upright, pyramidal tree displays glaucous green foliage and is possibly the most frequently seen of the named kinds.

—— 'Lutea'   syn 'Aurea'
A fine, slow-growing coloured foliage plant with sprays of clear golden leaves which later change to greenish yellow. Also sometimes seen are: 'Aureovariegata' with yellow banding on the green leaves with some sprays clear yellow; 'Variegata', or as it is sometimes called 'Argenteovariegata', in which the foliage is speckled with white.

—— 'Pendula'
Spectacular as a young plant, this beautiful upright tree has spreading horizontal branches from which the pale green branchlets hang curtain-like, in two rows.

Ch. obtusa   Hinoki cypress
ZONE 3

This is a timber tree of economic value in its native Japan and Taiwan, where under forestry conditions a height of 50 m (160 ft) can be attained, with their straight reddish brown trunks from 3 to

6 m (10 to 20 ft) or more in girth at the base. The foliage carried on crowded branchlets is rich green slighter paler on the reverse, thick and rather fleshy, leaves are scale-like and blunt-ended (obtuse). Hinoki have also long been cultivated in Japan as garden ornamentals. Several variations were imported into Britain by plant collector and nurseryman John Gould Veitch in the year 1861 and by others since. In spite of the fact that the species reaches a great height, most of the cvs we grow are either dwarf or in the medium-size range, almost all are suited to the average garden. Best results are obtained when planted in a moist lime-free soil. Propagation of the numerous sorts can be done by cuttings rooted under clear glass during the autumn. A great many of the plants sold are produced by grafting on to Lawson cypress rootstocks also done under glass, usually in late winter.

—— 'Albospica'
The white new growth of this dense, upright form is well displayed against the older green foliage.

—— 'Aurea'
A Japanese plant of typical pyramidal outline bearing flattened sprays of rich yellow foliage. It was introduced into Western cultivation about the middle of the last century.

—— 'Bassett'
Very rare, this small grower has deep green foliage on a small, rounded bushlet.

—— 'Caespitosa'
This mini-sized conifer is best grown in an Alpine house where the light green foliage which is carried on a bun-shaped plant is less liable to rot than when planted in wet outdoor conditions.

—— 'Chabo-yadori'
A recent importation from Japan with green foliage, both juvenile and adult type of leaves are present on the unequal length branches. Slowly builds into a rounded shrub.

—— 'Compacta'
An uncommon plant of conical form bearing deep green foliage.

—— 'Coralliformis'
The foliage is coral-like, twisting on the branchlets on this unusual sort.

—— 'Crippsii'
Open in growth when young this splendid form later develops into a small, sometimes broadly pyramidal tree. The golden yellow foliage is carried on elegant sprays which are spreading and have pendulous tips.

—— 'Fernspray Gold'   Pl. 39
A New Zealand raised clone in which the light yellow foliage is arranged in flattened, arching sprays. Slow growing at first but eventually forms a large bush of pyramidal outline.

—— 'Filicoides'
Unusual flattened sprays of dark green fern-like foliage on an open growing, rather untidy bush. Hard pruning is the answer, if done each year an interesting compact specimen will result.

—— 'Goldspire'
An upright, narrow, pyramidal tree with showy pale yellow new shoots which persist throughout the season. Introduced in 1963 by the firm of Messrs L. Konijn of Reeuwijk, Boskoop, Netherlands who have selected and produced many fine conifers in recent years.

—— 'Hage'
Another plant of Dutch origin. This eventually develops into a dense cone of bright green tiny foliage carried on slightly twisting sprays. A fine dwarf sort.

—— 'Intermedia'
This tiny gem forms a mound of light green leaves. It needs a well-drained spot well away from coarse rock plants to display best.

—— 'Juniperoides'
Compact dense bun. Another clone more suited to pot culture in a damp climate.

—— 'Kosteri' Pl. 23
One of the finest of the dwarf Hinoki, this has thick, shining deep green leaves arranged in cup-like sprays, often brown-tinged in cold weather. After many years this will form an upright, wide-based bush, seldom regular in outline.

—— 'Lycopodioides'
Another Japanese form which develops into a rounded, rather open, dwarf bush. The glossy green cord-like foliage is gathered into 'cockscombs' over much of the plant especially at the tips of the slender branchlets. 'Lycopodioides Aurea' is an even slower growing plant of similar style but with pale yellow foliage.

—— 'Mariesii'
Another dwarf. The dense pyramid shape is made up of light green foliage liberally dappled with creamy-white shoots.

—— 'Minima'
The tiniest of all the cultivated conifers easily confused with the heather *Calluna vulgaris* 'Foxii Nana'. It forms a dense pin cushion of light green foliage best displayed under cover or in a trough or pebble garden.

—— 'Nana'
Cultivated and revered by the Japanese for centuries and introduced to the West about 1860, this dwarf grower is now a favourite the world over. It very slowly grows into a rounded, flat-topped bush, the dark green foliage arranged cup-like in upwards-facing sprays.

—— 'Nana Aurea'
A first-rate, slow-growing golden form of the preceding plant but becoming upright and more open, eventually a small pyramid.

— — 'Nana Gracilis'
This plant with slightly twisting, shell-shaped sprays of glossy green foliage is the best loved and most frequently seen representative of the group. It is a most accommodating subject with many uses in the garden: a rockery plant, in the heather or pebble garden, a tub specimen, we have even noticed them used to form an attractive low hedge. Growth is slow, compact at first then broadly pyramidal.

— — 'Nana Pyramidalis'
Raised in the Netherlands from seed of the above and still a rare plant. Very slow in growth, the tiny cupped sprays of deep green are carried densely in horizontal layers.

— — 'Nana Lutea'   Pl. 24
This slow grower, the most colourful of the species, is more dense in habit than 'Nana Aurea' and eventually makes a tightly packed column of almost flat, rounded sprays of clear yellow foliage shading to white at the base. Our specimen is a charming sight when the winter-flowering heaths, with which it is planted, are in flower.

— — 'Pygmaea'
A distinct clone with light green leaves held on contrasting bright orange stems. The branchlets are arranged in more open 'fans' than most. Although the grafted plants normally offered are vigorous they do not get too large for most positions dwarf conifers occupy, but in time form a round, flat bush which turns rusty-brown in hard weather. 'Pygmaea Aurescens', a sport, bears sprays of yellowish green which have a permanent bronze tinge. A further clear yellow sport from the latter plant holds great promise for the future.

— — 'Repens'
Another sport, this time on 'Nana Gracilis'. It grows as sideways facing branched shrublet, almost prostrate, the light green leaves in tiny cupped sprays.

— — 'Rigid Dwarf'
A scarce plant which gradually develops into a tiny column of stiff upwards-facing branchlets bearing dark foliage and attaining under 1 m in twenty-five years.

— — 'Sanderi'
This slow-growing dwarf with entirely juvenile foliage is so unlike any other of the group that for many years it was considered to belong with the junipers. In summer the rather thick leaves carried on stout branchlets are sea-green but turn to rich purple at the onset of cold weather. A sheltered spot is suggested for this to succeed as it is less tolerant of cold than its fellows.

— — 'Spiralis'
Of stiff upright form, this slow grower bears contorted sprays of dark green foliage. A good selection for tub or trough.

—— 'Tetragona Aurea'   Pl. 36
This highly ornamental variety was received from Japan in about 1870. A slow grower but not really a dwarf unless restricted by regular pruning. The upright, rather open, branch system is clad with flattened sprays which terminate in crested or moss-like glossy pale golden-yellow foliage, deep orange at the tips when the weather is cold. A protected site for this one.

Ch. pisifera   Sawara cypress
ZONE 3

Introduced from Japan together with some of its cultivars, first to the Netherlands in 1859 and two years later into Britain, this species has produced from sports and seedlings a variable range of garden forms including many valuable dwarfs. The type is a rather uncommon tree in cultivation which has reached as high as 20 m (65 ft) in Britain but is seldom planted these days. The cvs are, however, popular. The species is conical with a fairly wide base when young, slowly assuming a tree of graceful habit. Clad with shining green to tawny yellow foliage, the level or somewhat pendulous branches sometimes layer themselves as they sweep the ground. Individual scaly leaves are rough to touch and have a resinous scent when crushed. The foliage is carried on reddish shoots—a colour also seen in the rough trunk. In its country of origin the aromatic timber is used for joinery purposes.

The cultivated plants fall into four reasonably distinct groups according to foliage type:

1 Adult—pisifera
2 Intermediate—plumosa
3 Juvenile—squarrosa
4 Thread-leaf—filifera

Propagation is from dormant wood under cool glass. Selection of the typical growth for increasing stock is important or an untypical plant can result.

—— 'Aurea'
A Japanese, adult foliage selection; commonly seen. Young leaves are golden-yellow later greenish as they age, the whole tree becomes yellow-bronze in cold weather.

—— 'Aurea Nana'
A slow-growing dwarf conifer of value in the rock garden where it forms a round-topped shrub of golden-yellow foliage.

—— 'Boulevard'   Pl. 29, 31
Introduced in 1934 as *Retinospora pisifera squarrosa cyano-viridis* by an American firm, Boulevard Nursery, this splendid plant has justly become one of the most popular of all garden conifers. Although eventually fairly tall—individuals of 6 m (nearly 20 ft) are on record—they are normally sold for use in the rock or heather

garden, their height being regulated by frequent trimming. The soft, light blue-grey foliage is seen at its best on plants growing in acid soils or in a cool greenhouse. In dry or windy places a partially shaded site is to be preferred. Not really suitable for soil containing much lime, the plants showing their displeasure by turning a dingy brown—at its worst in the winter.

— — 'Compacta'   Pl. 28
Slowly grows into a dwarf-rounded plant clad with curled sprays of blue-green adult foliage, distinctly white beneath and often brown-tinged in winter. This should not be confused with the much tighter 'Nana' which is described later.

— — 'Compacta Variegata'
Of similar shape to the above, although frequently looser in growth. This has gold or cream flecks and patches in with the green foliage. More attractive in cold weather when the variegation becomes pronounced. If either of the two cvs grow too open with age they can be lifted and replanted more deeply with the lower foliage resting on the soil.

— — 'Filifera'   Pl. 25
Growing into a wide-based bush or small tree this has long, spreading, pendulous branches with the branchlets whipcord-like carrying bright green leaves. Both this and its golden counterpart below form

impressive 'landscape' trees for the smaller garden. 'Filifera Nana' (Pl. 27) is a small, compact edition.

— — 'Filifera Aurea'   Pl. 26
The rather slower growing form of the above which has clear yellow stems. 'Golden Mop' is a dense, low grower seldom exceeding 1 m (3 ft).

— — 'Gold Spangle'   Pl. 29
Often also regarded as a dwarf this, although slow growing, has got to 5 m (16 ft). The lemon-yellow foliage is more adult in form than 'Filifera Aurea' the parent, some of the shoots hang in drooping congested bunches.

— — 'Nana'
One of the smallest of all the conifers, forming a low, tight bun composed of congested dark green intermediate and juvenile foliage.

— — 'Nana Variegata'
A form of the above with yellowish-green foliage, speckled with white variegation.

— — 'Plumosa'
This is an upright grower with a pyramidal outline. The bright green semi-juvenile feathery or frond-like leaves are less rough to the touch than those of the type. A good hedging plant which takes trimming well.

— — 'Plumosa Albopicta'
Similar to the above but with smaller, deep green leaves liberally spotted with white.

— — 'Plumosa Aurea'
Frequently seen, with bright yellow young leaves turning brownish in the cold weather. Dense, upright habit. Some nurserymen offer 'Plumosa Aurea Nana' which is a variable plant (probably different clones), similar to 'Plumosa Aurea' but slower growing. These golden plants are often confused with the following.

— — 'Plumosa Aurea Compacta'
Pl. 30
Dense, compact, rounded bush and although upright generally more broad than tall. Foliage colour as the foregoing but retaining the light yellow stage for longer, in warm countries the year-round.

— — 'Plumosa Compressa'
Pl. 34
The tiniest of plants, forming a tight bun of almost all juvenile foliage, which is pale yellow or greenish often with a blue tinge. The best examples are those which regularly have any projecting growth nibbled off with scissors.

— — 'Plumosa Flavescens'
Similar to 'Plumosa' except that in this form the leaves are yellowish-white tending to become green on shaded parts of the plant.

— — 'Plumosa Rogersii'
Dwarf, dense, developing into a perfect cone of soft, bright yellow, juvenile leaves. A first-rate rock plant on account of its bright colour and neat growth.

— — 'Snow'   Pl. 35
Developed in Japan, this forms a tight globe of light blue, moss-like foliage tipped and liberally flecked with white. The albino parts of the leaves suffer from scorch so much so that good specimens are invariably seen growing under glass.

— — 'Squarrosa' (often known as 'Squarrosa Veitchii')   Pl. 32
Pyramidal, the spreading branches have drooping tips. Dense, billowy, light blue-grey leaves are wholly juvenile and soft to the touch. Grown naturally this forms a large bush or small tree in time but can be kept much smaller by regular trimming.

— — 'Squarrosa Dumosa'
With its rounded shape this is a splendid dwarf, very dense blue-grey foliage which bronzes in hard weather.

— — 'Squarrosa Intermedia'
Pl. 33   syn 'Blue Dwarf'
A peculiar, yet when grown well, most attractive plant. It forms a dense, spreading mound of soft, light blue, juvenile leaves with partially reverted thread-like green shoots projecting from the surface. These have to be removed annually before they develop into disfiguring adult foliage and coarse stems.

— — 'Squarrosa Sulphurea'
 Pl. 38

Similar to 'Squarrosa' except for the soft sulphur-yellow foliage. This cv, raised in the Netherlands by Messrs Koster Bros (of Kosters blue spruce fame), needs a light, sunny spot to obtain the best foliage colour.

Ch. thyoides White cypress
 ZONE 3

A tree of pyramidal form endemic to the coastal regions of the southeastern United States where it attains some 25 m (80 ft). The very few plants of the type cultivated in Britain are relatively short-lived, seldom exceeding more than 10 m. Two different colour variations are grown, their fan-shaped branchlets bearing either green or blue-green leaves. This is a very hardy species which grows naturally in swampy ground, not really thriving where there is much lime present. The type can be increased from seeds; the few cvs from cuttings placed under glass in the autumn.

— — 'Andelyensis'
Raised in Les Andelys, France, over a century ago, this slowly forms an upright, usually very narrow column, the dense branches clad with very dark grey leaves in small fan-like clusters. Most attractive in early spring when liberally dotted with numerous tiny bright red male flowers. 'Andelyensis Nana' is a slower-growing plant over the years sending up many leaders and eventually making an extensive clump much more broad than high.

— — 'Aurea'
An upright, broadly conical plant of generally thin appearance. The pale yellow foliage is carried in the typical fan-like clusters on orange stems. The leaves become greenish at the onset of dull or wintry weather.

— — 'Ericoides'
This bushy plant with soft, juvenile foliage undergoes a colour change each season when the blue-green of the summer growth turns to rich purple with violet shoots during the cold season. A splendid contrast when planted with other slow growers especially those with golden foliage. Slightly sensitive to wind in exposed gardens.

— — 'Glauca'
A colour selection of the type which is grown for its glaucous grey leaves. Upright and slow growing of loose, open appearance it tolerates wet positions well.

— — 'Variegata'
Similar to the preceding but bearing bunches of clear yellow foliage as well as the normal grey. Although a good plant to have in a collection it tends to look rather sparse when grown in isolation.

× *Cupressocyparis*

A small group of hybrids between *Chamaecyparis* and *Cupressus* that have come about naturally only in cultivation. Leyland cypress, the only hybrid to be extensively planted, first came to light at the beginning of this century, although has only become generally popular in recent years. Propagation is from cuttings which can be rooted in sandy compost, under glass at almost any time of the year—late summer being preferred by ourselves.

× *C. leylandii* Pl. 45 Leyland cypress ZONE 4

These hybrids between *Cupressus macrocarpa* and *Chamaecyparis nootkatensis* are tall, spire-like trees with their foliage in flattened sprays similar to Nootka cypress but rather longer and more slender. The individual leaves are small, scale-like. Leyland cypress are of the greatest value for screening or tall hedges where a fast-growing evergreen is needed. They are also being used experimentally for forestry purposes where their hardiness and drought-resisting properties are put to the test. In this latter respect, a trial plot in a New Zealand Government establishment not only survived but actually put on new growth during a drought which killed *Pinus radiata* planted nearby. The early plants were raised in North Wales, clones have also come from Eire and Dorset, England.

— — 'Castlewellan'
A valuable, now established, favourite with golden yellow foliage.

— — 'Green Spire' (Clone 1)
Rapidly forms a column of bright green foliage.

— — 'Haggerston Grey' (Clone 2)
One of the two sorts most commonly planted, this has dark grey-green leaves arranged in dense, irregular sprays.

— — 'Leighton Green' (Clone 11)
The second frequently seen plant, very similar to the above in general appearance but some consider this form the easier to root.

— — 'Naylors Blue' (Clone 10)
Seldom listed, but well worth searching for this has a greyish sheen to the young leaves.

— — 'Stapehill'
This arose independently of the others and was introduced in 1940 by Messrs Barthelemy's Nursery, Stapehill, Wimborne, England. It grows into a thin column, the brown stems carrying light green foliage.

Cupressus

The cypresses are ornamental evergreen conifers, most of which have slender upright growth when immature becoming more open as they age. They are much valued in milder areas for screening, giving protection from sun and wind. The true cypresses are generally less hardy, especially when young, than the members of *Chamaecyparis* with which they are often linked. Protection from cold wind is therefore suggested until the plants are established. Adult foliage is minute, scale-like, pressed tightly to the stems; juvenile more open, feathery. The cones are relatively large, rounded, usually ripening in their second year but remaining on the tree for several seasons after the seed is shed. Species raise readily from seed sown either in pots under glass or in a sheltered spot outside. Although not easy to root, the cvs are increased by placing cuttings under glass during the summer. Nurseries sometimes graft choice kinds in late winter using seedlings of *C. macrocarpa* as stocks. Because of their sparse root system many individuals do not transplant readily as large plants and for this reason pot-grown are to be preferred.

C. cashmeriana Kashmir cypress
ZONE 8–9

An elegant, upright branched tree of pyramidal outline with cascading branchlets of light grey—almost white—foliage in flattened sprays. Unfortunately, one of the least hardy of the group and unlikely to succeed out of doors except in virtually frost-free parts of the world. Here it will make a superb specimen tree.

C. funebris Mourning cypress
Chinese weeping cypress
ZONE 8–9

This tree, as well as being a native of Central China, is also frequently planted there. Formerly used for conservatory decoration in Europe, when young juvenile foliage seedlings were chosen for their soft, bright blue leaves. Older plants bear flattened sprays more like the *Chamaecyparis* group in appearance.

C. glabra Arizona cypress
ZONE 6

This species is usually sold as *C. arizonica*, a similar but rarer sort. Forming a dense pyramidal tree, its stout trunk clad with reddish bark and ascending branches of light silver-green foliage, it is a fine plant for a hot dry position and reasonably hardy once established.

— — 'Aurea'
A broad-based, pyramidal tree with yellow-tinged foliage. 'Golden Pyramid' is an improvement with richer colour display, a very dense, upright column.

— — 'Hodgins' syn 'Hodgins Variety' or 'Hodginsii'
Strong growing with open branches densely clothed with hard, light silver-blue leaves. An outstanding cv developed by Messrs Hodgins Bros, nurserymen, of Melbourne, Australia.

— — 'Pyramidalis' Pl. 41 syn *arizonica* 'Conica'
The most popular of the group which quickly forms a spire of light blue foliage. 'Blue Pyramid' is a refined version, recently introduced.

— — 'Variegata' Pl. 40
This rare plant has bold patches of white foliage against the typical blue. It requires a sheltered place to protect the albino portions from the scorching effect of wind and sun.

C. lusitanica Mexican cypress or Cedar of Goa ZONE 8

Rapid growing, valued for screening purposes in warm temperate areas. Upright trunk with reddish bark, spreading branches and grey foliage in drooping sprays. The attractive cones are bright glaucous blue changing to brown as the seeds ripen. A plant long cultivated in cold glasshouses in Britain for its decorative young foliage; it was thought at first that it was a native of either Portugal (Lusitania) or Goa, the former Portuguese colony in western India, but is now known to be a wild plant of Mexico.

— — var *benthami*
This Mexican tree is a distinct form, now possibly more often planted than the type due to its neater habit of growth. It is narrowly pyramidal with the grey leaves carried in frond-like sprays.

C. macrocarpa Monterey cypress ZONE 7

This the most hardy of the cypresses has a restricted distribution as a wild plant in Southern California but is very common in cultivation. This is no doubt due to its usefulness for screening and is nowhere more valued than in coastal areas for filtering salt-laden winds. Growth is rapid, upright and pyramidal when young, often gaunt in old isolated specimens. The green rather thin adult foliage is only seen on these old plants which have been left to develop naturally. Clipped young stock tends to retain the juvenile, soft form of leaf. Unfortunately, too rare to be listed here are some fascinating miniature clones which are seldom listed by specialist nurserymen. Propagation of the species is easy from seed. They can be sown three or four to a small pot and then thinning one to a pot after germination. Cvs root from cuttings, sometimes with difficulty.

— — 'Aurea'
Upright, dense, with spreading branches this bright golden plant was raised in Australia and like all clones displaying this colour needs to be placed in full sunlight to develop the richness of tone. 'Fine Gold' and 'Sunshine' are two excellent conifers of recent years which appear to come into this group.

— — 'Conybeari' syn 'Aurea Saligna'
A most unusual, large growing, bushy plant of light golden foliage arranged on long, drooping, cord-like stems recalling a thick-stemmed thread-leaf Sawara cypress in form.

— — 'Donard Gold'
Raised by the Slieve Donard Nursery Co of Newry, N. Ireland, this develops into a dense column of rich yellow foliage. A great improvement in form over 'Lutea', the original golden-yellow version. 'Goldcrest' (Pl. 42) raised by Messrs Treseders of Truro, Cornwall, England is a gem for any garden, the rich yellow hue of the feathery foliage intensifying during the cold weather. Recalling the fastigiate Italian cypress in form but not colour are 'Gold Cone' and 'Golden Pillar'.

— — 'Horizontalis Aurea' Pl. 44
Also formerly listed as *lambertiana* 'Aurea' by Australian and New Zealand nurserymen, this plant is of the brightest yellow-gold with the dense foliage produced on horizontal or slightly ascending branches. A striking specimen for lawn or foundation planting.

— — 'Lutea'
Tall, pyramidal, rather open-topped grower with light yellow new leaves which change to pale green by the autumn. Except for where a large specimen is required this has been superseded by the brighter colour, more compact growers (*see* 'Donard Gold' above).

C. sempervirens Italian cypress
ZONE 7

This native of southern Europe is a variable plant with two distinct main forms, one with spreading branches and the other a slender column. Some botanists believe that the former is the original wild plant and others call it var *horizontalis*. Both in gardens and when growing in a truly wild state, this is often seen as a flat-topped tree, usually with a wind-swept appearance. The second main form is also seen growing naturally, its dark spires being a feature of parts of the Italian and Greek countryside. Their foliage resembles that of *C. macrocarpa* but is finer with smaller individual scale-like leaves.

— — 'Stricta' Italian cypress
A narrowly fastigiate column of

dark green seen at its best in a poor well-drained warm soil. With its formal outline many garden uses can be found: a tall specimen or avenue, as a hedge that needs no clipping or even as a patio or tub plant. This is a group name that covers all the narrow, upright forms for seedlings come mostly true to type. Not hardy in Britain as a young plant, although in sheltered gardens they gain hardiness with age.

—— 'Gracilis'
This cv of the Italian cypress which was raised in New Zealand is said to be a more refined version with soft green leaves. Being only increased from cuttings and not from seed, an even stock is assured—most important if a neat formal hedge is to be planted.

—— 'Swane's Golden' Pl. 43
Raised by Messrs Swane Bros. Nurserymen of New South Wales, Australia this is a light yellow,

pencil-slim version of the Italian cypress. Tending to be slower growing than the green form this is suited to even the smallest garden.

C. torulosa Bhutan cypress
ZONE 8

An eventually large tree from the northern Himalayas and western China, selected clones of which quickly make symmetrical specimens for lawn planting in warm temperate countries. The foliage is dark green and is arranged in flattened sprays as in the False cypresses, carried in bunches at the ends of the ascending branches.

—— 'Corneyana'
More pendulous than the type with the branchlets arranged irregularly. The tree develops into a neat conical shape when mature.

Juniperus

Evergreen conifers of variable habit which ranges from prostrate ground-hugging shrubs to large bushes and small trees. Some of the trees are large enough to be of timber yielding size. As the wild species occur mostly in the northern hemisphere they are almost all hardy in the British Isles and countries with similar climate although some may require a little protection until established. The aromatic leaves are awl- or needle-shaped when in their juvenile state and usually prickly. The adult foliage is scale-like and clasps the stems more tightly. Both forms of leaf frequently appear together on a plant, some (particularly the Common juniper) retaining more juvenile foliage, even when mature. Almost all of the junipers make good garden plants, especially where space tends to be limited and more naturally dwarf plants occur in this genus than any other. Also worth noting is the fact that several wild species choose to make their home on chalk or limestone and do well in similar soils in cultivation although it does not appear to be essential for their well-being. Any reasonably well-drained soil will suit them either poor or fertile; the upright forms as specimens or in a mixed border, low growers on banks and rockeries. The two sexes of flower can be either carried on one tree or on separate individuals according to species. The cones or fruit look like berries and are really composed of fleshy scales; they often ripen in one year but sometimes take two. The seeds which remain viable for many years are erratic in germination and for this reason cuttings are normally used for increase of stock. Grafted plants are sometimes offered by nurseries, but as cuttings root so readily when placed in sandy compost under glass during the autumn, it is a method of increase best left to the professional.

J. chinensis Chinese juniper
ZONE 4

A variable, generally tall species from China and Japan with upright, columnar or pyramidal form. The type, of which examples are seldom seen, has greygreen leaves, juvenile as well as adult appearing together—even on old trees.

— — 'Aurea' Young's Golden Chinese juniper
A very dense conical form with clear yellow-gold foliage. Although eventually tall, it is slow enough to be used in most gardens with good effect.

— — 'Japonica'
Dwarf, dense and very prickly to handle with most of the branchlets clad in sharply pointed juvenile leaves together with a few projecting semi-weeping shoots of adult scale-like foliage. The plant varies in colour from rich green to yellowish the whole with a glaucous sheen.

— — 'Kaizuka' syn 'Torulosa' Hollywood juniper
An attractive plant with more or less upright branches and irregularly clustered branchlets of rich green leaves. Interesting specimens can be formed with selective pruning. 'Kaizuka Variegata' or 'Variegated Kaizuka' is of note for its bold splashes of yellow against the grey-green normal foliage.

— — 'Obelisk' Pl. 59
A narrow, upright column of densely set blue-grey juvenile

leaves. This forms a small tree of value as a focal point in the heather garden or can be planted in a shrub tub to decorate a patio.

— — 'Oblonga'
This is a prickly shrub which grows in a rounded shape, and as it was originally a sport of 'Japonica', it can be regarded as a dwarf form of that plant.

— — 'Pyramidalis' Pl. 65
A fast-growing subject of narrow conical shape. The juvenile leaves are glaucous green and very prickly. Like other plants of this group they need an open situation in which to develop best, planted closely they tend to become bare on one side due to the spread of the fungus botrytis on the foliage.

— — 'San Jose'
With grey-green, predominately juvenile leaves, this is a valuable hardy, almost prostrate cv.

— — 'Stricta'
Particularly neat in shape this forms a dense cone of soft, light blue-grey juvenile leaves. A splendid addition to the heather garden.

— — 'Variegata' syn 'Abovariegata'
This conical bush has patches of white-splashed foliage.

J. communis Common juniper
ZONE 2

A hardy, variable species is found over a wide range in the northern hemisphere. The foliage is wholly juvenile, awl-shaped, rather prickly. Male and female flowers are on separate plants, the latter bearing crops of blue-black berries from which, before they ripen, the well-known flavouring for gin is extracted.

— — 'Compressa' Pl. 55
This extremely slow-growing tiny green column is a favourite for the smallest rock garden or scree.

— — 'Depressa Aurea' Pl. 62
A dwarf-spreading plant with drooping, clear yellow new shoots. These turn to old gold by the autumn and in cold weather the whole plant assumes a purple-bronze hue.

— — 'Depressed Star'
Similar in general appearance to the foregoing but with entirely light green shoots and foliage. This is a selected clone of the sub-species from Canada, var *depressa*.

— — 'Hibernica' Pl. 61 Irish juniper
The familiar, dense, slender column of deep green foliage. These are suitable for formal situations where they develop naturally without trimming. Also at home in the heather garden where the slim, upright shape breaks the flatness of the low mounds of the other planting. Cold, windswept sites should be avoided.

— — 'Hornibrookii' Horni-
brook's juniper
At first prostrate but building up
in time to form a low, mounded
bush. This is a justly popular
dwarf plant with tiny, green silver
backed leaves. Splendid when
perched atop a low wall allowing
the young stems to trail down
naturally.

— — 'Repanda'
Rapid growing, dwarf carpeter
suitable for using as fairly extensive ground cover. The dark
greyish-green leaves, soft to
handle, are carried on semi-
prostrate brown stems. The original plant was a wild 'find' in
Ireland by the late Maurice
Pritchard of Christchurch, Dorset, England.

— — 'Silver Lining'
This attractive little plant has
completely prostrate stems which
hug the ground each strong
growing shoot clad with shining
green leaves. The apt name coined
by Mr H. J. Welch of the Wansdyke Nursery, Devizes, Wiltshire,
England refers to the silvery
reverse to the tiny leaves some of
which are twisted to reveal their
'silver lining'.

— — 'Suecica' Swedish juniper
A variable plant, typical specimens of which are similar to the
Irish juniper in their upright
growth, but usually more open at
the top with many projecting
shoots. 'Suecica Nana' is un-

common, in appearance much
like a larger version of 'Compressa'.

— — 'Vase' syn 'Vase Shaped'
An open-centred plant with
branches ascending at an angle.
The grey-green leaves often turn
deep bronze in the winter.

J. conferta Shore juniper ZONE 5

This Japanese species is found
growing wild in sandy sea-coast
locations. Prostrate, dense growth
with slightly ascending brown
stems and large, soft, pale green,
needle-like leaves.

J. davurica ZONE 3

Said to be widely distributed in
northern Asia, little is known of
the type plant although its cvs are
commonly planted.

— — 'Expansa'
A low-spreading plant made up of
clusters of rich, green juvenile
foliage with projecting stems of
adult-type leaves.

— — 'Expansa Aureospicata'
Similar to above, but with bold
yellow markings to the mainly
juvenile leaves.

— — 'Expansa Variegata'
Another variegated clone, this one
more vigorous than the foregoing.
The white portions contrast
beautifully against the rich green
of the normal leaves. Both the
variegated sorts are liable to 'burn'

when the plants are sited in hot sun.

J. horizontalis   Creeping juniper
ZONE 3

A North American species, variable in the wild, all are low growing most being prostrate. The branches are extremely long, branchlets dense—usually short, foliage awl-shaped or scale-like, blue-grey in colour.

— — 'Bar Harbor'
Thin trailing leading shoots, side branchlets held upright. The grey-green leaves assume a delightful mauve tone in cold weather.

— — 'Douglasii'   Waukegan juniper
Prostrate, strong-growing clone which forms a dense mat of stems with glaucous-green leaves which turn light purple in winter.

— — 'Montana'
Of similar grey-blue colour to the popular 'Wiltonii' below, but with the short branchlets held upwards rather spreading over the soil.

— — 'Plumosa'   Andorra juniper
Rather taller than most in this section with the procumbent stems rising at the ends. Dense, soft grey leaves turn purple in the winter. A fine introduction of the Andorra Nursery Co., Philadelphia, USA.

— — 'Wiltonii'   syn 'Blue Rug' or 'Wilton Carpet'
This much planted trailing shrub is at first completely prostrate, later the blue-grey stems mound slightly in the centre. This is the same plant as 'Glauca' of the European nurseries and is invaluable where a dense, low carpet of growth which smothers weeds with its strong outgrowing shoots, is needed.

J. × media   van Melle's hybrid juniper   ZONE 4

A name which covers a group of (apparently) natural hybrids between *J. chinensis* and *J. sabina*. Although there is considerable variation between its members, they fall roughly into two sections: the 'Plumosa' type with rather stiff, more or less upright branches clad with mainly adult, scale-like leaves. These are like their Chinese parent in many respects. The important 'Pfitzerana' group are more savin-like with branches carrying a mixture of foliage and arching out from the short trunk to form a wide, spreading bush. Some writers do not recognise these distinctions and group them all under *J. chinensis*.

— — 'Blaauw'
A most attractive plant originally imported from Japan. The thick, reddish, upright branches are clad with clustered grey-green

leaves and thin projecting young shoots. 'Plumosa' section.

— — 'Gold Coast'
An exciting recent development from 'Pfitzerana Aurea' with almost entirely yellow leaves which deepen to rich gold in cold weather.

— — 'Hetzii'   Pl. 64   Hetz
    juniper
Where a large, fast-growing shrub is needed this will be a good choice. Bearing masses of light grey foliage it is adaptable to most types of soil and will also take heavy pruning by branch removal. Eventually large, but can be contained easily.

— — 'Old Gold'
A sport of 'Pfitzerana Aurea', rather slower in growth than its parent, the delightful golden colour is retained well throughout the year, becoming 'old' gold in winter.

— — 'Pfitzerana'   Pfitzer's
    juniper
One of the most useful of all conifers for its quick growth and adaptability. The long, densely clothed branches of deep green foliage grow up and outwards before drooping at the ends with the weight of the mass of leaves. The bush builds itself up layer upon layer as the years go by and where space permits it will eventually cover a wide area. 'Mint Julep' is a derivation with clear light green leaves; 'Pfitzerana Compacta' as its name suggests is more dense with firm adult green leaves, a handy plant where the others in this section would grow too large; 'Pfitzerana Glauca' is a refined version of 'Hetzii' with low branches and very prickly. Superb 'blue' plant.

— — 'Pfitzerana Aurea'   Pl. 67
    Gold Pfitzer
At first a dense, low bush but later taller with the mature foliage glaucous green and clear yellow, drooping new shoots. Very colourful and easy to grow.

— — 'Plumosa'   Chinese plume
    juniper
A dwarf grower with upright branches often naturally inclined to one side. These are clothed with short branchlets of stiff, dark green leaves.

— — 'Plumosa Aurea'   Gold-
    dust juniper
This yellow version of the Plume juniper ultimately gets very large. The side shoots of pale yellow leaves arch outwards from the long spreading branches.

J. procumbens   Pl. 57   Creeping
    juniper   ZONE 5

A vigorous spreading plant from Japan with stiff, prostrate branches of blue-green leaves which are arranged in threes on the branchlets. A useful mat-forming species valued for covering bare soil.

— — 'Nana' Pl. 58 syn 'Bonin Isles'

The D. Hill Nursery Co. of Dundee, Illinois, USA introduced this splendid compact grower from Japan. Procumbent except for its slightly raised leading shoots, the leaves are a particularly fresh shade of green becoming slightly bronzed during the winter. A well-grown plant always commands attention when well sited on the rock or pebble garden.

J. recurva Drooping juniper
ZONE 7

A large tree in the wild but in cultivation this species from the eastern Himalayas is generally seen as a tall bush. The bark peels in reddish strips, branchlets are drooping clad with grey-green leaves.

— — var *coxii* Pl. 66 Coffin juniper

This distinct subspecies was introduced from mountainous Upper Burma. It develops into a small, thin tree with drooping branches and branchlets of green or slightly grey foliage. Also retained for many seasons are the clusters of reddish dead leaves. Young specimens require training to secure an upright stem.

— — 'Embley Park'

Distinct from the type this low-growing plant was raised from seed sent from China by that great plant hunter George Forrest. When newly expanded the pointed leaves are a particularly bright shade of fresh green.

J. rigida Prickly juniper or Needle juniper ZONE 5

This is a beautiful small tree from Japan with greyish bark, spreading branches and elegant drooping branchlets. The individual leaves, which are well separated on the shoots, are prickly, greenish in colour and marked with grey bands beneath. The round fruits are black covered with a grey bloom.

J. sabina Savin or Sabin juniper
ZONE 4

This variable, long cultivated shrub from mountain areas of Europe and Asia has a spreading branch system with the stems usually upright clad with green or grey leaves. These are nearly all scale-like, adult in form, but the softer, awl-shaped juvenile type are also sometimes seen, all have a peculiar odour when crushed in the hand. The plant sold by nurserymen under the species name is the Dutch Savin juniper, *J. sabina* 'Erecta'. They make good garden plants, some on the rock garden, the vigorous spreaders are suitable for ground cover when planted fairly thickly in rough places.

154

— — 'Arcadia'

This low grower with slightly raised branches clad in rich green leaves was raised in the United States from seed imported from Russia.

— — 'Blue Danube'

Low growing or shrubby, the branches clad with light grey leaves spread over the ground, rooting as they grow.

— — 'Hicksii'

This particularly vigorous clone is frequently used for extensive ground cover. The branches, partially erect at first, are well furnished with grey leaves which turn dark mauve at the tips in winter.

— — 'Skandia'

With the same origin as 'Arcadia' this hardy, low spreader with light green leaves is also first rate ground cover.

— — var *tamariscifolia*
   Tamarix juniper

The best clone of the Spanish form of Savin is known as 'Tamariscifolia' (Pl. 60) and is extremely popular as a rock garden specimen or as edging to a flight of steps. The prostrate branches of light blue leaves build up layer upon layer until a dense mat is formed.

— — 'Variegata'

White portions appear with the dark green normal foliage on this upright branched, spreading shrub.

— — 'Von Ehren'

An open, many-stemmed bush which eventually develops into a large mound—the better for a trim over with the hedging shears now and then.

J. sargentii   Sargent's juniper
ZONE 5

Originally discovered growing on the sea-coast of northern Japan by Prof. Sargent who sent material to the Arnold Arboretum, Massachusetts, USA. This is a slow-growing juniper which is completely prostrate in growth, and as well as thriving in poor soil, is disease resistant too. The adult leaves are light green in the type, clones vary from this colour to glaucous blue.

J. scopulorum   Rocky Mountain juniper   ZONE 5–7

A small, narrowly pyramidal tree of western North America usually seen with several trunks springing from near the base. Branches are thick, branchlets slender with small scale-like leaves. Foliage colour varies both in the wild plant and in the many named clones recorded, only a very small selection of which are given below.

— — 'Blue Heaven'   syn 'Blue Haven'

A fine selection which has neat, compact, upright habit and foliage of clear light blue.

—— 'Gray Gleam'
Forming a neat, rather narrow cone of grey leaves and retaining its colour the year-round, instead of changing to dull purple in the winter as do some of the others.

—— 'Hillborn's Silver Globe'
A rounded, irregular mass of silver-grey foliage.

—— 'Pathfinder'
This has silvery leaves on flat sprays and is a narrow column on maturing.

—— 'Platinum'
A broad-based, dense pyramid of shining silver leaves.

—— 'Springbank'
Upright, tall, rather thin in appearance with the light blue of the summer colour tending to turn a little drab at the onset of cold weather.

—— 'Tabletop' syn 'Tabletop Blue'
This spreading, leader-less bush has startling clear blue foliage. It makes a better plant with denser growth when the leading shoots are reduced in length during alternate seasons.

J. squamata Scaly juniper
ZONE 4

As is common to many plants having a wide distribution in the wild, this is a variable plant; some are small trees—others low spreaders. The branches are generally stout, branchlets short with drooping tips, leaves large and carried thickly.

—— 'Blue Star' Pl. 56
This is a splendid recent introduction with intense silvery-blue leaves in which the trunk is absent, the branches developing into a dense low mound of spiky appearance.

—— 'Meyeri'
Introduced to the West many years ago from a Chinese nursery garden, this now popular subject has large steel-blue leaves. It is usually seen as an upright shrub and with training will grow into an interesting small tree. The retained dead leaves can detract from the elegance of the drooping shoots so should be removed with care when possible using hands protected with strong gloves.

—— 'Wilsonii'
Often treated as a dwarf subject, this plant of either open or dense conical shape (there are possibly two forms in cultivation) can get large in time. The dense green foliage is well marked with two almost white bands above.

J. virginiana Pencil cedar or Eastern Red cedar ZONE 4

North America is the natural home of this hardy, small tree. As its common name implies, the aromatic red wood has a commercial use in the manufacture of pencil casings. In cultivation, the plants seen are more bush-like with upright trunk, branches at first ascending, thin branchlets with small, sharp, scale-like adult leaves predominating with clusters of more open juvenile type here and there. Many more cvs are planted than the selection given below.

— — 'Burkii'
One of the better selections with steel-blue adult and juvenile leaves, purple in winter. Habit is upright, dense, columnar.

— — 'Canaertii'
A narrow pyramid of dark green leaves with new shoots projecting from the dense mass of upright branches. Regular fruiting is a feature, the branchlets bearing crops of bloom-covered berries.

— — 'Schottii'
One of the more common tree-like forms with branches of light green leaves.

— — 'Grey Owl'   Pl. 63
A favourite, this develops into a billowy mass of thin branchlets clad with tiny grey leaves. It is often regarded as an intermediate between *J.* × *media* 'Pfitzerana' and *J. virginiana* 'Glauca' but is normally regarded as a cv of the latter. For isolated specimens or tallish ground cover.

— — 'Skyrocket'
All of the branches are strictly ascending on this, one of the most exciting of all conifers to appear in recent years. Their extremely narrow spires of silver-grey foliage are a welcome addition to the garden finding many uses both formal and informal.

Thuja

A small group of evergreen shrubs and trees allied to, and closely resembling, the flat-leaf cypresses from which they differ chiefly in their egg-shaped cones with overlapping scales. The foliage, aromatic if bruised, is scale-like in the species but some cvs retain the juvenile seedling type throughout their life. Together with juvenile forms of other members of the Cypress family, the latter were at one time accommodated in a genus of their own; called *Retinospora*, it is a name sometimes still seen in catalogues. Their soil preference is for a well-drained moist site where specimens develop into shapely plants, very dense, usually conical in form. The species as well as many of the cvs are fine hedging plants and in addition there are several slow-growing kinds suited to the rock garden. Male and female flowers are on different parts of the same tree, their cones containing a few seeds in each ripen late in the year; they are used to increase the species.

Sowing takes place (preferably under glass) during the spring and the young seedlings potted on when large enough to handle. They are finally grown on in a nursery plot before planting in their permanent place at 0·5 m (1½ ft) tall or so. Cuttings of both species and cvs can be rooted in a frame by inserting in sandy compost during the autumn. Rare kinds have been grafted in the past using seedlings of the type as understocks. The common name originally given to *Thuja occidentalis* was Arbor-vitae. It means 'tree of life' and is seldom used except in books and catalogues, the Latin *Thuja* being preferred.

Th. koraiensis Korean Arbor-vitae ZONE 5

This Korean plant is usually seen as a bushy shrub, in other forms older specimens grow into a slender, less dense column. Their strongly scented foliage is arranged in fan-like sprays and is blue-green in colour and bears whitish bands beneath.

Th. occidentalis American Arbor-vitae or White cedar ZONE 2

Variable usually tall very hardy tree from eastern North America with glossy green or pale yellowish-green foliage, usually turning brown in the winter. There are some fine garden forms including several dwarfs. As a hedge plant the type with its much divided leaves is useful but not nearly as good as *Th. plicata* when used for this purpose.

— — 'Alba' Queen Victoria Arbor-vitae
This grows to a neat pyramidal shape and has pure white tips to the flat sprays of foliage.

— — 'Aurea'
Broad-based and bushy with yellow leaves.

— — 'Beaufort'
Raised by Mr W. Haalboom, a nurseryman from Driebergen-Rijsenburg, Netherlands, this develops into a slender, open-branched pyramid with the dark green leaves boldly variegated in white.

— — 'Caespitosa' Pl. 48
Compact, bun-like mound of tiny stems clad with green, mainly adult leaves. All too rare, this would make a charming addition to any rock garden.

— — 'Columbia'
From an early start as a loose bush, this becomes columnar in outline. With white tips to the pale green leaves the most spectacular effect is seen on young vigorous plants during the winter.

— — 'Ericoides' Pl. 37
Soft juvenile type of foliage, grey-green when in growth it becomes pale brown in winter. Normally seen as an ovoid shrublet, often

158

with several leaders, the weak stems will be flattened by snow resulting in permanent damage unless quickly removed.

— — 'Fastigiata'
A dense, often narrow, upright growing clone of regular shape which has its use as a neat specimen.

— — 'Globosa' syn 'Tom Thumb'
The light green-grey foliage on densely packed branchlets forms a perfect rounded shape on this low grower.

— — 'Hetz Midget'
Tiny, very slow-growing ball of green foliage on much reduced stems. Originally discovered as a seedling in an American nursery.

— — 'Holmstrup' syn
'Holmstrupensis'
A narrow column of rich green, sometimes brown-tinged leaves held in tight vertical sprays. Although growing large in time, it never becomes unmanageable.

— — 'Little Gem' syn 'Green
Globe'
This popular dwarf grows into a ball of small stature. The dark green foliage is carried on flat, slightly twisted sprays.

— — 'Lutescens' Pl. 46 syn
'Wareana Lutescens'
A dense, slow-growing pyramidal shrub of distinction. The shoots and large flattened sprays of foliage are cream or pale yellow for their first season later becoming pale green within the plant.

— — 'Ohlendorffii'
Raised near Hamburg, Germany at the end of the 19th century, this unusual clone consists of grey, juvenile foliage arranged neatly in four rows on the shoots with thin whipcord stems of scale-like adult leaves projecting from the ovoid bushlet. Annual removal of the latter is advised in order to maintain its form.

— — 'Rheingold' Pl. 53
A dwarf, broadly conical plant with a mixture of the two types of leaves, the juvenile feathery sort present at the base of the flat adult stage branchlets. The colour varies with the seasons from pale yellow with the young tips pink, later orange to rich old gold in winter. Its intense colour is always most welcome in the garden, but never more than when lightening dull days. Some people reserve the name 'Rheingold' for the smaller, often rounded, entirely juvenile plants (maintained by removal of older leaves if they form) and use the name 'Ellwangerana Aurea' for the taller, more common plant.

— — 'Smaragd'
A useful, upright, pyramidal plant of dense habit with its dark green foliage retained the year-round—a useful point to remember if a hedging subject is being selected. Raised in Denmark.

159

—— 'Vervaeneana'
Tall growing, this was originally a Belgian plant. It forms the typical pyramid shape of the group but has its dark green leaves marked and tipped in white. Often turning brown in cold weather then pale green in its second year.

—— 'Wansdyke Silver'
Dwarf and densely pyramidal with dark green foliage and creamy-white variegation retained well.

—— 'Wareana'
Upright, compact, vertical branches of bright green foliage in large sprays.

—— 'Woodwardii'
Another dwarf-rounded plant composed of spreading and ascending branches of bright green which becomes brown-tinged in winter. The attractive ball-shape is kept without trimming.

Th. orientalis Chinese Arborvitae or Biota ZONE 6

A tree of moderate size from northern and western China which is frequently planted in its homeland and Japan. In the Western world better known for the small, usually extremely neat, bush-like forms. The type species is sometimes seen growing as an old specimen. These have a short trunk, which has patches of shiny bark, bare upswept branches and

large-domed crown of light green foliage held almost vertically, in flattened, yellowish-green sprays. For garden decoration the golden sorts are some of the best coloured conifers we have in the small-to-medium height range.

—— 'Aurea Nana' Pl. 52
Berkman's Arbor-vitae
A first choice for many, this superb little plant develops into a fat, ovoid bushlet of dense upright foliage sprays, light yellow-green in colour.

—— 'Beverleyensis' Pl. 50
Dense, upright, eventually columnar in outline with its bright golden-yellow outer foliage tinged red-brown at the onset of winter wind and cold.

—— 'Conspicua' Pl. 49
Upright, symmetrical grower, eventually fairly tall and certainly worth planting where an ultimate height of 3–4 m (about 15 ft in as many years) will not be too large. The golden-yellow fresh growth is particularly bright.

—— 'Filiformis Erecta'
A most unusual acquisition which grows into a loose, round bush of coarse whipcord-style stems of green foliage tipped yellow when in spring growth.

—— 'Juniperoides' Pl. 51 syn *Thuja decussata*
Considering the appearance of this plant with its soft, retained juvenile leaves—so unlike the nor-

mal thujoid foliage—it is not difficult to understand why botanists took many years before deciding where to place this and other variants of similar appearance. A sheltered spot is suggested for these forms, their grey foliage liable to damage in the cold of winter. The colour of this particular dwarf plant is superb during the autumn when it assumes a rich purple tone.

— — 'Meldensis'
Another small grower with dense juvenile foliage. Eventually an ovoid or ball-shape, its leaves are green-grey when in growth, violet in winter.

— — 'Rosedalis' Pl. 54 syn 'Rosedalis Compacta'
A third dwarf also with juvenile leaves and generally rounded habit. This is less dense than the others and is soft—the other two have a crisp feel about them. The plant changes colour with the seasons, clear yellow new shoots mellowing to pale green then finally grey-purple in the winter.

Th. plicata syn *Th. lobbii*
Western Red cedar ZONE 5

A very tall forest tree in western North America where the timber is highly valued for building uses. In gardens it grows into an elegant pyramidal tree with reddish-brown trunk and spongy bark, highly aromatic glossy green leaves clothe the spreading branches. The species, which succeeds best of all in a slightly moist but well-drained soil, withstands clipping well and for this reason is frequently used for hedging as well as screening.

— — 'Atrovirens'
A selected clone with particularly rich shining green leaves.

— — 'Cuprea'
Dwarf, dense, rounded bush of short branchlets with foliage-coloured cream or deep gold on the extremities. A superb rock garden specimen plant.

— — 'Hillieri'
A very hardy, slow-growing, rounded bush of irregular length branchlets clad with tufts of thick, grey-green leaves which bronze in hard weather.

— — 'Old Gold' Pl. 47
This vigorous upright form is popular in New Zealand where it was raised. The bright golden colour is maintained well through the seasons only bronzing in cool areas. A satisfactory hedge plant.

— — 'Rogersii' syn 'Aurea Rogersii'
A popular very dwarf rock plant of dense conical form. The tiny leaves are golden-yellow tipped with orange, bronzing in cold weather when it is at its best.

— — 'Stoneham Gold'
Eventually tall but very slow growing this broadly conical

shrub is suited to the heather or large rock garden. The light golden yellow new foliage appears even brighter as it contrasts with the dark green of the centre older leaves.

—— 'Zebrina'
An upright, broad pyramid in which the green leaves are clearly marked with zebra-like banding of gold and cream on the young growth. So heavy is the variegation that the tree appears to belong to the yellow cvs when viewed from a distance.

Thujopsis

A Japanese tree formerly included with *Thuja*, but now accorded a genus of its own. The evergreen foliage of the single species is large, carried on peculiar, green plastic- or ribbon-like branchlets, deep shining green above, white beneath. Although eventually reaching tree-like proportions, from the garden point of view they are best treated as shrubs and pruned as needed to keep them within bounds. Unless grown in isolation they tend to lose their lower branches but pruned or given plenty of space they remain furnished to the ground. The method of obtaining new stock is similar to other members of the family with cuttings rooting with ease if they are placed in sandy compost, under glass during the autumn.

Th. dolabrata ZONE 6

The type species described above.

—— 'Aurea'
An uncommon kind with leaves of pale golden-yellow.

—— 'Nana'
A good low grower which being reduced in stature makes a wide, flat-topped bush of rich green which bronzes in hard weather.

—— 'Variegata'
White variegated foliage with the colour in patches, some parts more so than others, a point to be remembered when selecting wood for propagating.

PINACEAE   Pine family

Abies

The Silver firs are found in mountain areas of central and south-west Europe, Japan and North America. Some forty species are at present recognised, many of them of great economic importance and almost all eventually forming imposing specimens. Some of the wild plants are among the world's taller trees with individuals of over 100 m (more than 300 ft) on record. The best trees are those growing in deep moist soils in areas of high rainfall. Unfavourable conditions include shallow, dry, or (with some notable exceptions) chalky soils. Additionally some suffer from late spring frost—especially when young. The great height of many of the wild trees need not preclude the use of several species in the garden where growth tends to be more slow anyway. Their shape is symmetrical, conical in outline when young with a whorled tier of branches added annually. In the tall growers these lower branches eventually fall away leaving a straight, smooth trunk with branches radiating from the crown. The evergreen, frequently glaucous leaves are linear, almost flat with conspicuous white stomatic bands visible when viewed from below or when branches are lifted in a breeze. They are arranged in two different ways: on leading growths they are radially around the shoot, on side branchlets usually in two opposite ranks. Winter buds of leader shoots, their shape and whether resinous or not, the general appearance of the new growth and also cones are the means the expert has of distinguishing between the species, some of which were included with *Picea* at one time. The flowers appear in the spring with the numerous male flowers composed of a catkin-like cluster of red or yellow stamens carried on the sideshoots, the females nearer the tip. The upright clusters of fertile cones expand during the summer, some change from green to violet or yellow. In the autumn these all turn brown and break up while still on the tree—almost as soon as they are ripe, with the seeds and scales falling together. Propagation is from seed which must be sown as soon as practicable as they do not remain viable for long. The cvs are increased by grafting on to seedlings of the closest species using leading shoots as scions for side growths are difficult to train up to form a trunk and usually develop into a lop-sided plant.

A. alba European Silver fir
ZONE 4

A common tree of upland slopes in mountains of central and eastern Europe. Starting life with a pyramidal outline with branches to the ground but later when very tall it has a bare trunk and rounded crown. The smooth bark is greyish when young, scaly in old age. Foliage dark green above, white beneath; winter buds are small and brown. Cones brownish-green before maturing to rich brown.

A. amabilis Red Silver fir ZONE 5

This is a tall growing tree from western North America with an attractive, almost white trunk. The long leaflets are deep green above with white bands beneath; buds are globular and very resinous. Cones purple when young.

— — 'Spreading Star'

A prostrate growing form, the original specimen of which is in the Blijdenstein Pinetum, Hilversum, Netherlands. This would make a useful garden plant which could eventually cover a large area with dense growth.

A. balsamea Balsam fir ZONE 3

A variable tree found growing wild in Canada and the north-eastern United States its mature height depending on the climate of the particular location. The bark is smooth, greyish and covered in resin bumps and is the commercial source of Canada Balsam used in medicine and optics. Leaves are shining dark green above with greyish tips and grey bands beneath; buds reddish, resin-covered. Violet when young the cones are also resinous.

— — 'Hudsonia' Pl. 70

A dwarf plant of distinction forming a dense flat-topped globe of branchlets clad in short foliage. 'Nana' is similar at first glance but carries its foliage radially instead of semi-radially as in 'Hudsonia'. Both are very hardy and particularly tolerant of alkaline soils.

A. cephalonica Greek fir ZONE 5

An attractive tall tree of pyramidal form found at altitudes of around 1500 m (5000 ft) among limestone rocks in Greece. The densely set, broad leaves are stiff, sharply pointed, dark green with white reverse; buds pale brown and very resinous. Cones long and narrow, greenish-brown at first.

A. concolor Colorado fir or White fir ZONE 4

A beautiful tree and accommodating garden plant which is a native of western United States where old specimens of up to 60 m (200 ft) occur. The trunk is grey, smooth when young, clad with branches to the ground. The rather thick, long leaves are variable in colour, either green or glaucous, arranged both in opposite rows and also standing above the shoot. The cylindrical cones are green often stained with purple. Some interesting spreading plants can be obtained by propagating side branches of selected silver-leaved seedlings. The usefulness of this species is extended by its tolerance of dry soils.

—— 'Candicans'
One of the best silvery-white foliage forms of all the conifers.

—— 'Compacta'
Slow-growing dwarf cv of irregular, compact outline which has striking grey foliage.

—— 'Glauca Prostrate'   Pl. 73
Attractive plants with silver-grey leaves, low growing.

—— var *lowiana*   Pacific White fir
This naturally occurring subspecies has smaller winter buds, shorter branches and a more open crown than the type. The grey leaves are arranged in opposite or in two V-shaped rows.

—— 'Violacea'
Selected for its striking silver-grey foliage.

—— 'Wattezii'
Pale yellow new foliage becoming silvery with age. A tree of only moderate size and although unusual, not really as good as silver kinds.

A. delavayi   ZONE 7

Of Chinese origin, this is a variable tree the type species of which seems to be very rare in cultivation.

—— var *forrestii*   Forrest's fir
An attractive tree of moderate stature from western China. The reddish stems bear shining deep green leaves with white reverse; buds are almost round, covered in white resin. A notable feature of the plant are the conspicuous dark purple cones.

A. fargesii   Farges fir   ZONE 5

This pyramidal tree is also from China. Vigorous with long branches, the generally smooth shoots are orange-brown tinged with purple, dark green leaves carried thickly in two or more rows. Winter buds are large, conical and very resinous. Cones purplish at first.

A. grandis   Grand fir   ZONE 6

This American species is fast growing in deep moist soil, and although eventually reaching a great height, it is most attractive in the garden as a young plant. Growth is narrow conical with the rather thin shoots carrying leaves, unequal in length, deep shining green above, silver beneath, in two rows. Buds are small, almost round, resinous. Cones greenish-brown.

—— 'Aurea'
A form in which the leaves have a yellow tinge.

A. homolepis   Nikko fir   ZONE 5

An adaptable species which is a native of Japan. Grows to a large size even under difficult soil conditions. The shoots are deeply grooved, yellowish in colour, densely clad with leaves that are green with white bands beneath; conical buds are resinous. Cones are very long, purple before maturing to brown.

A. koreana   Korean fir   ZONE 5

This splendid alpine species is noted for its neat manner of growth and early coning. Pyramidal in form with thick, pale brown shoots clad with stiff green leaves, silver beneath. The very attractive cones which are deep violet in colour come as a surprise bonus on a young plant.

A. lasiocarpa   Alpine fir   ZONE 3

Slow growing although eventually tall this tree from western North America is pyramidal or conical in shape. The short grey-green leaves spring from downy shoots; small winter buds are brown and resinous. Cones are narrow and cylindrical, purple in colour.

—— 'Compacta'   Pl. 69
Possibly a clone of the subspecies *arizonica* the Cork fir, this is a superb, slow-growing plant of broadly conical shape. The silvery-blue leaves with white reverse are densely arranged on the short branchlets with the resinous winter buds particularly noticeable.

A. magnifica   Californian Red fir   ZONE 5

A large growing forest tree of narrow pyramidal outline which is a native of the western USA. It is seen at its best when growing in deep, moist soil and is not adapted for alkaline conditions. The brownish shoots are downy, long leaves blue-green carried thickly on the upper side of the branchlets; round buds slightly resinous. The long cones purple when young.

—— 'Glauca'
A selection with brighter grey-green leaves.

A. mariesii   Maries fir   ZONE 5

Found in Japan, this tree of moderate to large size has a slender, pyramidal outline. The trunk is grey with stout branches carrying downy reddish branchlets with the shiny green leaves bearing two white stomatic bands beneath; small winter buds are resin-covered. Oval cones are violet-purple until ripe.

A. nordmanniana   Caucasian fir   ZONE 4

This is a variable, always large

grower often of broadly pyramidal shape with long sweeping branches on old specimens. The grey-brown shoots are slightly hairy with the deep green leaves white-banded beneath. The foliage is densely arranged above the shoots, opposite below; winter buds are brown and not resinous. Long, ovoid cones are greenish when young.

— — 'Pendula'
This kind has wide spreading branches with drooping tips.

— — 'Golden Spreader'
A very choice, pretty, dwarf cv with clear yellow leaves.

— — 'Prostrata' syn 'Procumbens'
Wide-growing plants produced by propagating the sideways-facing branchlets.

A. numidica   Algerian fir   ZONE 5

A rare wild tree of moderate size which is sometimes met with in cultivation and which is of value for its tolerance of city air. Habit is pyramidal with a regular branch system, shoots greenish-brown, dark green leaves arranged around the stem—most facing forward or up; large winter buds resinous at first. The long cones are brown in colour.

— — 'Pendula'
A slow grower with its pendulous shoots bearing the typical thick, almost bristle-like leaves.

A. pindrow   West Himalayan fir or Pindrow fir   ZONE 6

A tall tree generally of narrow pyramidal shape with a graceful appearance and one seen at its best when growing in a cool climate. The smooth young shoots are stout, yellow-brown with the very long leaves of bright green loosely arranged and mostly hanging below the shoot; winter buds are slightly resinous. The greenish-brown cones are cylindrical in shape.

— — var *brevifolia*   ZONE 7
This differs from the type in general appearance and has reddish-brown shoots and shorter, stiff, pale green leaves.

A. pinsapo   Spanish fir   ZONE 6

This distinct species can be seen growing in a few mountain areas of south-west Spain, where it is a protected wild plant. An adaptable garden tree of only moderate size for many years it is one of the few Silver firs that really do well in chalky or dry soil. Shoots are smooth, reddish-brown with deep green leaves radiating all around; winter buds ovoid, resinous. The cylindrical cones are purple-brown.

— — 'Aurea'
A low-growing shrub with insipid pale gold foliage.

— — 'Glauca'   Pl. 71
A large grower with striking

glaucous blue foliage. Raised in France in the late 1800s, the true plant can be raised from graftings only and blue seedlings which appear from this plant, although desirable garden subjects, have no right to the original name.

A. procera syn A. nobilis Noble fir ZONE 4

This slender, tall tree from the western United States is of note for its remarkably dense leaves and beautiful cones. Although too tall for many gardens, the species makes a superb specimen where it is allowed space for development. Young shoots are covered in rust brown, downy hairs, leaves are short, blue-green with pale bands beneath; buds resinous. The greenish-yellow cones are the largest of all the firs and are particularly attractive.

—— 'Glauca' Pl. 72
One of the most desirable of conifers with intense silver-blue foliage. Always grafted, the plants are variable in shape, the best being from leading shoots. Our illustration shows a crop of large cones carried on a specimen no more than 2 m (6 ft) in height growing in a front garden in Boskoop, the nursery area of the Netherlands. When side shoots are selected for scions spreading plants are the result. Such a plant is 'Glauca Prostrate'.

A. veitchii Veitch's Silver fir ZONE 3

A beautiful tall tree which was discovered in Japan and introduced into Britain as long ago as 1861 by J. G. Veitch, head of the then famous nursery firm of that name. Young shoots are covered in reddish-brown down, soft, dark green leaves are conspicuously silver on the reverse. They are carried thickly and curve slightly upwards; buds purple. The sessile cones are cylindrical, bluish-purple in colour.

Cedrus

The cedars are a small group of distinctive evergreens well-known for the majestic ancient specimens to be seen in parks and large gardens. The value of their fragrant wood has been appreciated since early times and was formerly considered an important commodity of trade. Their tiny needle-like leaves are carried in two ways: spirally on the young leading shoots and in tufts on short spurs arranged on the mature branchlets. A slender pyramid when they are young the trees develop with a massive, often black trunk with wide, spreading branches. Their soil preference is for a well-drained sandy loam which remains moist during drought conditions. On mature trees the autumn-flowering male catkins are most prominent. No less conspicuous as they mature, either on the same tree or as separate individuals, are the large oval cones carried above the sweeping or upright branches. These ripen in two years then break up while still on the tree. Some taxonomists have, in the past, regarded all the cedars as one species, individuals being simply geographical variations. They are certainly very similar and difficult to identify with accuracy when mature. Cedars can be raised from seed but all named kinds have to be grafted under glass during the early spring. Seed should be sown in gentle warmth to ensure an even germination.

C. atlantica Atlas cedar ZONE 6

A familiar, eventually large tree from the Atlas Mountain range in North Africa. The branches ascend strongly in a young plant but later they become more spreading although almost always the pointed crown is retained. Very old trees are remarkably like *C. libani* but seldom have such extensive flat areas of foliage.

— — 'Aurea' Golden Atlas cedar

Golden leaves shorter than the type. Pyramidal in shape it is not as robust as the green sorts but in good soil will provide a satisfactory specimen.

— — 'Fastigiata'

Raised in Nantes, France in 1890 this cv has shoots which are reduced in length and branches that, in a young plant, ascend rigidly upwards before filling out to form a narrow pyramid. A popular clone, frequently planted and one which is usually supplied as *glauca* for the foliage, is a similar blue-green.

— — var *glauca* or 'Glauca' Blue cedar

With glaucous blue foliage the year-round, these are one of the most popular of conifers for isolated specimens. The name covers a group of plants for 'blue' forms occur in the wild as well as from seed in cultivation. A typical plant is large growing, with the ascending branches bearing white-blue leaves.

— — 'Glauca Pendula' Weeping Blue cedar

When carefully sited this is a tree of rare beauty displaying long weeping branches covered with glaucous blue foliage. The best specimens are those which have been obtained by grafting into a stem at least a man's height from the ground.

— — 'Pendula' Weeping Atlas cedar

We have seen this small weeping

tree grafted low down—where it has made a charming subject as its stems of green foliage trail along the ground.

—— 'Pyramidalis'
Raised in 1889, this is a distinctly pyramidal tree of French origin sometimes still listed by conifer specialists.

C. brevifolia   Cyprus cedar
ZONE 7

The mountains of Cyprus are the natural home for this small growing cedar, which is the least common of the four species. Often treated as a dwarf, plants are seen in pots or in restricted pockets in the rock garden. Given space and good soil they tend to grow much larger but never the size of the Deodar which they resemble.

C. deodara   Pl. 74   Deodar or Indian cedar   ZONE 7

This eventually very tall Himalayan species is an elegant tree at any age. They are variable from seed and many named sorts are the result. All have pendulous branches clothed with light grey or grey-green needles some of which measure up to 5 cm in length. Mutant forms have also appeared with clear yellow leaves.

—— 'Albospica'
A rare tree with white tips to the young growth but rather inclined to 'burn' in hot sun.

—— 'Aurea'   Golden deodar
During the spring this splendid plant has golden yellow foliage on all exposed leaf surfaces. As growth matures the colour mellows to greenish-yellow. Of value in the smaller garden not only for the colour but also for the slow rate of growth and smaller ultimate size.

—— 'Aurea Pendula'   Pl. 68
More pendulous than the foregoing, this has leaves coloured yellow-green in the summer, bright gold in winter.

—— 'Pendula'   Weeping deodar
Although frequently seen as a completely prostrate carpeter with shoots lifting up at the ends, this can be stem-trained upwards to produce an attractive small weeping tree.

—— 'Pygmy'
Collectors of dwarf conifers think highly of this really tiny grower the original of which was discovered growing in a Californian nursery in 1943. It forms a hummock of rather spiky, glaucous needles.

—— 'Robusta'
A strong-growing pyramidal form with the pendulous tips of the wide-spreading branches hung with long blue-green needles.

C. libani   Cedar of Lebanon
ZONE 5

This is the familiar slow-growing tree of our parks and large gardens. Young specimens are pyramidal in shape gradually becoming flat-topped with age. The widespread branches of clear green foliage sometimes suffer damage during heavy falls of snow and should be propped where possible.

— — 'Comte de Dijon'
A miniature of conic form with much reduced branchlets and shoots of sharp-pointed, sea-green needles.

— — 'Golden Dwarf' syn 'Aurea Prostrata'
Yellow foliage—brightest in the winter, small size and with the horizontal branches sometimes held prostrate on the ground—mark this plant as unique among the Lebanon cedars.

— — 'Nana' Dwarf cedar
A choice rock garden plant, compact, pyramidal in shape, much reduced in all its parts including the sharp, blue-green needle-like foliage.

— — 'Pendula'
A rare tree of moderate height with distinctly narrow weeping branches.

— — 'Sargentii'
This weeping plant which originated in the Arnold Arboretum, Boston, USA is eminently suited to a position of honour on the rock garden where its shoots bearing blue-green needles can radiate from the short trunk to cascade over a rock face. It should be possible to train a specimen up a stake to form a small pendulous tree.

— — var *stenocoma*
Forming forests in South-West Anatolia, Turkey, this is considered by botanists to be a separate geographical race. In cultivation they appear as intermediates between *C. libani* and *C. atlantica* with silvery foliage and pyramidal in shape when young, becoming flat-topped in older specimens.

Larix

The larches, one of the few genera of deciduous conifers, are not only of great value for the timber they produce, but also for garden ornamentation. There are about ten species known, yet apart from those used in forestry few are in general cultivation; the less common kinds are seen only in arboreta or private collections. Those described below are rapid growing and apart from the weeping cvs, conical when young. They form a straight trunk; old specimens usually lose their lower branches and form a wide, spreading crown. Carried on pendulous shoots, the needle-like young foliage—much like the cedars in form—is always a welcome sight as it heralds the spring, the autumn colours of yellow or old gold are no less beautiful. In the garden their main use is for screening or planted in groups to form a shelter belt. They do well on most soils including poor sandy or gravel but dislike badly drained sites. Male and female flowers are on the same tree, the female catkins very showy when open on the bare twigs in spring. Their cones mature the first season and although the seeds are shed when ripe the empty cones remain on the twigs for some time afterwards. Seeds are used to increase the species, they should be sown in a well-drained, warm soil in early spring. As they are so fast growing transplanting for forestry purposes takes place after only one year. For the garden those of two years are more usual, older transplants are not always successful. Cultivars are increased by grafting on to established seedlings—a very specialised procedure. None of the very attractive dwarf clones are in general cultivation.

Larix decidua European larch or Common larch ZONE 2

Cultivated for many years and a tree much used in forestry and of value in the garden where a fast-growing screen is needed. Young specimens are cone-shaped with whorled branches. From these spring the pendulous yellow shoots with bright green needle-like leaves which turn dark green in the summer then clear yellow in late autumn.

— — 'Pendula' Weeping European larch
Weeping forms of the species have been found both in the wild and in gardens. The finest specimens are those that are obtained by grafting in scions at a height of 2 m (6 ft) or more to allow the long pendulous shoots to hang gracefully.

L. × eurolepis Dunkeld larch or Hybrid larch ZONE 4

These are the result of hybrids between *L. decidua* and *L. kaempferi* first noticed at Dunkeld, Perthshire, Scotland around the year 1900. Because of their hybrid vigour and resistance to disease they have become popular forest trees, usually outstripping both of their parents in growth rate.

L. kaempferi Pl. 104 Japanese larch ZONE 7

Another fast-growing larch frequently planted, particularly in the western counties of the British Isles. Its ultimate height, although 30 m (over 100 ft) or more, is not as tall as the European larch from which it also differs in its more glaucous summer foliage, which turn to buff-yellow before falling.

—— 'Pendula'
A beautiful, tall growing weeping tree with bluish-grey foliage raised in Germany during the last century. Unfortunately, this splendid form is all too rare in cultivation.

Picea

The spruces are a large genus of evergreen trees often found in vast forests over much of the northern hemisphere. Many of these are valued for their timber and turpentine, a by-product. Young plants are normally pyramidal in outline with their branches arranged in tiers. Older specimens become, in some species, more open-branched with their trunks exposed. Their foliage is narrow, often hard, needle-like carried on small 'cushions'—tiny growths on the stems which remain after the leaves have gone which give the shoots a characteristic 'raspy' feel. Male flowers are in the form of round catkins, either red or yellow; fertile 'flowers' on the same tree develop into clusters of drooping cones which ripen in one season. When mature, these open to allow the winged seeds to drift away leaving the empty cones (complete with scales) on the tree to fall later. Several of the species are very ornamental garden plants, the large growers for specimens or screening; especially valued for smaller sites are the many dwarf and coloured-leaf kinds. Propagation of the species is from seed sown outside during the autumn or in the spring. Cuttings of many sorts (including most of the dwarfs) root if placed in a closed frame during late summer. Grafting of choice kinds is done each year by experts and this is not a job for the inexpert.

P. abies syn *P. excelsa* Norway spruce or Common spruce
ZONE 5

This is a wild plant in central and northern Europe and also a familiar forest tree in Britain and elsewhere. When immature, it is also known as the Christmas tree. The shiny green leaves are carried densely on grey or reddish shoots. Cones are cylindrical, up to 15 cm (6 in) in length, carried in clusters. This species of spruce has, over the years, produced the greatest number of variations, only a small selection of those named in the past and still offered by nurserymen are described below.

— — 'Acrocona'
An eventually tall bush with spreading or drooping branches and which have bright red cone-like flowers on almost every branch tip in the spring—even on a young plant. It also bears normal cones.

— — 'Aurea'
Light yellow young foliage, in some plants this soon turns to green, but in others deep gold or striped. A valuable addition for colour contrast in a collection of taller growers.

— — 'Clanbrassiliana'   Lord
    Clanbrassil's spruce
One of the earliest of dwarf conifers. Compact and dense, it eventually grows into a wide-topped bush. Many of the plants in commerce are said to belong to 'Clanbrassiliana Elegans', a similar but rather quicker growing sort.

— — 'Cranstonii'
Of British origin, this small pyramidal tree—first recorded in 1855 —has a very open appearance due to the almost total lack of side branchlets on the main branches.

— — 'Echiniformis'   Pl. 82
    Hedgehog spruce
A low grower which forms a dense mound of congested shoots which end in a mass of buds and long, spiny, dark green forward-facing needles.

— — 'Gregoryana'
Sometimes confused with the above, but when mature this is the smaller of the two. It is extremely slow growing—our specimen is only 0·3 × 0·5 m (1 ft × 1½ ft) after owning it for twelve years— with pale green, sideways-facing small needles.

— — 'Inversa'   Drooping spruce
With its branches hanging almost straight down, this is an intriguing form when a vertical trunk is maintained by training; left to its own devices it sprawls.

— — 'Little Gem'   Pl. 77
The name of this very tiny grower is almost self-explanatory. Raised in the Netherlands from a sport on 'Nidiformis' it grows into a round mop-like bushlet of very short, bright green leaves.

— — 'Nidiformis'   Pl. 80
    (Birds) Nest spruce
A familiar variant with rounded, spreading shape; the top with its central depression suggesting the common name. This disappears on an old plant.

— — 'Ohlendorffii'   Pl. 76
    Ohlendorff spruce
Another slow-growing, frequently planted small spruce. The small leaves are yellow-green, the sharply pointed buds bright orange.

— — var *pendula*
A botanical name sometimes used by gardeners; it covers several clones (many named) with weeping branches.

— — 'Pendula Major' Weeping spruce

A strong growing, pyramidal tree. The graceful drooping branches are seen best when it is planted in isolation on a lawn.

— — 'Procumbens' Prostrate spruce

This is a low, wide, spreading plant with plenty of vigour. Use it in the rock garden or front of a mixed border.

— — 'Pumila Nigra'

A most attractive cv with dark, shiny green leaves and prominent orange winter buds. It is slow growing having its stiff branchlets angled outwards.

— — 'Reflexa'

This strong grower has normal foliage on pendulous branches but is completely without a trunk unless one is formed with training. Never better than when rambling over rocks in the larger alpine garden.

— — 'Remontii' Remont spruce

This gradually develops into a regular cone-shaped plant of yellowish-green leaves. Slow growing, it takes many years to attain 3 m (10 ft).

— — 'Repens' Creeping spruce

A prostrate carpet, regular in outline where given space. Dense, spreading, building up in the centre in time.

P. brewerana Pl. 75 Brewer's spruce ZONE 2

A beautiful tree, very rare in the wild where it is confined to a few places in the Siskiyou Mountains of the Californian/Oregon border area. Growing to a medium size only and therefore suited to most gardens, growth is upright, broadly pyramidal, its sweeping branches bearing very long pendant banchlets of blue-green needles. Some patience is needed but rewarded when the plant has reached the size of the magnificent specimen 'rising like a green fountain' growing in the Great Park, Windsor, pictured in the illustration.

P. engelmannii Engelmann spruce ZONE 2

Although growing to 50 m (160 ft) in the wild, this dense pyramidal tree from the Rocky Mountains of western North America is normally much smaller when seen in cultivation. Very hardy and growing in many soils except chalk, the soft grey leaves ending in a sharp point are arranged above the pinkish-brown shoots. Cones are oval or cylindrical, green with a purple flush. The cv 'Glauca' has a better, lighter grey colour than the type.

P. glauca White or Canadian spruce ZONE 2

This tall, very hardy species

comes from Canada and the north-east of the USA where it is an important forest tree used for milling. Of value for its hardiness and the ability to flourish in bleak situations, it develops into the pyramid shape typical of the group, has long spreading branches which ascend at the ends, leaves are light green, ending in a horny point. Cones are narrow, cylindrical, blunt-ended.

— — var *albertiana* 'Conica' (see below).

— — 'Conica' Pl. 81
This popular slow-growing form is everyone's favourite for its neat cone shape and bright green foliage. Originally found in the wild, they are now distributed around the world. Regular attention during the spring and early summer with a suitable insecticide is important if an infestation from red spider mite—a common foe— is to be avoided.

— — 'Echiniformis'
A fine dwarf plant which appeared in France in 1855. It makes a flattened, globular bush of small shoots clad with forward-facing, grey-green needles.

— — 'Nana'
This is a rounded dwarf bushlet of stiff branchlets of blue-grey leaves.

P. jezoensis Yeddo spruce
ZONE 4

A very tall tree from central and

northern Asia usually represented in gardens by the var *hondoensis* Hondo spruce. This is an erect grower of neat symmetry with its foliage silvery on one surface and dull green on the other. On a mature plant the bright crimson male flowers are an added attraction. This tree makes a fine lawn specimen which does not suffer the spring frost damage of the type.

P. likiangensis

An interesting Chinese tree of rather open habit of growth attaining 20 m (65 ft) in cultivation. It is represented by two vars.

— — var *likiangensis* Likiang spruce ZONE 5
Long spreading branches with ascending ends. Leaves flattened, sharply pointed, blue-green on one surface, white on the other. Prolific flowering in the spring with conspicuous red catkins; cones reddish when young.

— — var *purpurea* Purplecone spruce ZONE 5

A tree of rounded shape with thick spreading branches. The rich purple cones are an attraction in summer.

P. mariana syn *P. nigra* Black spruce ZONE 2

Found in Alaska, Labrador, Michigan and Newfoundland, this varies in the wild from a tall tree to dwarf-stunted bushes according to altitude. They are generally pyramidal in outline with whorled branches clad with bluish-green leaves. The cones are dark purple when immature and remain on the tree for up to thirty years after the seeds are released.

— — 'Doumetii' Pl. 86
Although eventually reaching 5 m (16 ft), this is regarded as a slow grower developing into a wide-based pyramidal or round-topped bush. The spreading branches are densely set with thin, silvery-green needles.

— — 'Nana' Pl. 79
A dense rounded, compact plant with radiating shoots bearing glaucous-blue leaves. Our plant (Pl. 79) is still only 0·3 m × 0·5 m (1 ft × 1½ ft) after being purchased as an established plant and being with us for twelve years.

P. omorika Pl. 84 Serbian spruce ZONE 4

There are few finer sights in the conifer world than a group of these slender trees rising spire-like from their surroundings. Of extremely narrow form, their pendant branches curve upwards at the ends. Leaves are deep green and silver; cones are small, coni-cal, dark purple when young. The species has a very limited range in Jugoslavia where they grow in acid accumulations in limestone rocks.

— — 'Expansa'
An unusual plant clad with nor-mal size foliage, yet almost pros-trate and wide spreading, the branch ends ascending.

— — 'Nana' Dwarf Serbian spruce
A compact, very dense shrublet. Wider rather than high, with small pale green leaves which are turned to display silvery bands.

— — 'Pendula'
A selection with the drooping branches held closely to the trunk. Their foliage is grey-green, softer than the type.

P. orientalis Eastern spruce or Oriental spruce ZONE 4

A tall pyramidal tree from the mountain slopes of the Black Sea area. They are similar to *P. abies* in general outline, but are more compact and have considerably shorter leaves. These point for-ward and are arranged semi-radially above the brown shoots. The narrow cones are long and purple when young.

— — 'Aurea Pl. 85 syn 'Aureospicata'
A startling sight when the bright cream new shoots appear each spring; these later change to gold and finally fade to pale green al-though the bush retains a golden aura the year-round. Older needles are deep green on this tall bush.

— — 'Gracilis' Columnar
Oriental spruce

This is normally seen as a bush of dense shoots covered with bright green leaves. Older specimens are tall, narrowly upright or pyramidal.

P. polita Tiger-tail spruce or Japanese spruce ZONE 5

A Japanese tree with horizontal branches which forms a broadly pyramidal specimen. New shoots are stout, cream changing to buff, leaves long, sickle-shaped with hard, very spiny tips. Cones are solitary, long, yellowish when young. Suitable for planting as an isolated specimen, its main interest lying in the long, dark green curved leaves.

P pungens Colorado spruce or Blue spruce ZONE 2

Specimens of over 30 m (100 ft) are recorded in the mountains of western United States where the tree grows naturally. They are seldom as high in cultivation where the fine glaucous foliage forms are more common. Because of their brilliant colouring these named clones are some of the most desirable of conifers suppliers being hard put to meet the demand for established specimens. Their more-or-less radially arranged leaves are curved, thick and prickly, carried on stout white or orange shoots. Branches are in horizontal whorls, the tree developing into a broad-based pyramid when young later having crowded branches towards the crown and a bare trunk. Cones are pale yellow. The group as a whole (including seed-raised stocks of the type) contains valuable garden ornamentals, especially when in their early life they are vigorous with branches to the ground. They thrive in dry and normal soils, but are particularly prone to attack by Red spider mite in the former.

— — 'Compacta' Dwarf
Colorado spruce

A dense bush with all its parts reduced, the horizontal branches clad with grey-green foliage. One of the older named kinds which was raised from seed collected in the wild.

— — 'Glauca' Blue spruce

This is the collective name for all glaucous seedlings, found in the wild or raised in gardens from seed. They are usually slower growing and generally less tall than the normal form of the species. Although attractive, with foliage colour varying from silver-green to blue-green, better colour is seen in the many-named clones.

— — 'Glauca Prostrate' Pl. 83
Prostrate Blue spruce

This is the name used for a group of valuable garden plants which have come about (either by accident or design) as the result of grafting a low side branch usually taken from a named clone. Mr Welch calls these 'cultivariants' and the way that they grow in a one-sided fashion, as though they were still part of the original tree, gives a clue to their origin. When these are derived from a naturally pendant grower, such as 'Koster', they are very attractive plants indeed.

— — 'Endtz'

Introduced by a Dutch nurseryman; grows into a broad pyramid with the stiff horizontal branches clad with deep blue needles.

— — 'Globosa'   Pl. 78

A rounded bush composed of small shoots bearing bright blue needles. The plant photographed in the Pygmy Pinetum, Devizes, Wiltshire, England shows that this is ideal where a small size is preferred.

— — 'Koster'   Koster's Blue spruce

An erect pyramid with slightly drooping branches. This is the best known of the Blue spruces, its intense silvery-blue leaves and neat shape have made it the universal favourite.

— — 'Moerheimii'

Another popular plant sometimes sold as 'Koster'. This too has brilliant blue leaves and grows into a dense bush of rather more upright branches.

— — 'Pendula' syn 'Glauca Pendula'

This uncommon plant has the familiar bright foliage colour of the best of the group, but with a strange manner of growing. Having a weak trunk and usually curved, it makes a plant that is neither upright nor completely prostrate. Branches sweep the ground, for both branches and the branchlets are pendulous with raised tips.

— — 'Thomsen'

One of the finest, with long rather thick leaves which are shining white-blue and carried on stout branchlets which develop into a specimen of perfect symmetry.

P. sitchensis   Sitka spruce   ZONE 6

A large tree from western North America used for forestry purposes in Britain and elsewhere. It is also valued where a fast growing, yet ornamental screening subject is needed. They thrive in a wide range of soils, including those almost permanently moist, but intolerant of dry sites or frosty hollows. Pyramidal with branches in whorls, branchlets long, clad with prickly green needles marked with white beneath. Cones are long, cylindrical, curved, yellowish at first.

P. smithiana   Morinda spruce or West Himalayan spruce   ZONE 6

This very tall-growing species is known to attain 60 m (200 ft) in the wild, generally less than half that after a great many years in cultivation. The maturing specimens rival the beautiful Brewer's spruce in their elegant sweeping branches that are furnished with long pendant branchlets. The needles are long, shining dark green, where the plants are growing well and are arranged radially around the pale cream shoots. Unsuitable for frosty places; a fine specimen kept losing new spring growth after we moved it from the mild west of England to a new site near London.

Pinus

Occurring over most of the northern hemisphere, the pines are one of the best known ornamental and economically important groups of conifers. The many species range in height from low bushes to tall trees. Because of their variability they are assured a place in gardens large or small. Frequently conical in outline when immature, trees normally develop a single trunk which is invariably of attractive colour and form. The leaves are of two types: small, papery, scale-like and deciduous appearing with the new shoots—and the much more prominent evergreen needles. The needles are usually in clusters of two to five joined together in a sheath, six to eight in one species, or carried singly in some sorts. These needles are almost always very dense on the branchlets persisting for several seasons before falling. The pollen-bearing male flowers are red or yellow; female flowers on the same tree are woody and later develop into cones. After the pollen has fallen on the open scales of the female flower, these close, although complete fertilisation may not take place until almost a further year has elapsed. Once fertilised the cones grow rapidly to various sizes according to the species, normally ripening during their second year. Seeds are not always released when mature, some being retained within the cone for a good many seasons.

In addition to the quantities of millable timber produced annually from the pine, other products include rosin, turpentine and pitch from the resin; leaves yield commercial pine oil when distilled and the seeds—pine kernels or piñones—are edible in many species.

A rather poor, well-drained acid soil suits them best although in such a large genus of nearly one hundred species, individuals can be found able to thrive in almost any soil and situation. Seeds are used to propagate all the species, choice kinds placed under glass during the spring making sure that the emerging seedlings are shaded from the hot sun. Alternatively, they can be started in spring by sowing directly in drills outside, transplanting to a nursery bed a year later. A few species and cvs can be rooted from cuttings, although the majority that cannot be raised from seed have to be grafted under glass using pot-grown seedlings of the appropriate group: *P. sylvestris* for the two-needled sorts and *P. strobus* for the others. Most pines resent root disturbance so should be grown on in containers until ready to site or else planted out in their permanent position when still young. Given the choice between a tiny well-balanced seedling and a large one (probably coarse-rooted plant), the former is to be much preferred.

P. aristata Bristle-cone pine
ZONE 5

This is an extremely long-lived alpine species from the southwest United States. Although eventually attaining 10 m (over 30 ft) or more, its growth is slow enough for it to be used on a rock garden. Branches are upswept with thin, crowded leaves in bundles of 5, curving forward on rust-brown shoots. Blue-green outer needles are heavily spotted with resin which, from a distance, gives the impression that the tree is under attack from some kind of insect pest.

P. armandii Armand's pine
ZONE 5

An attractive tree from the mountains of China, Taiwan and Korea reaching some 20 m (65 ft) in the wild, generally smaller in cultivation. The trunk is grey, branches spread in layers, smooth yellowish branchlets bear thin,

light grey-green needles with white reverse in fives. When young much like the better known *P. wallichiana*.

P. ayacahuite Mexican white pine ZONE 8

A beautiful, large tree from Mexico and Guatamala which grows to 25 m or more (over 80 ft) in mild localities. The spreading branches bear long greyish needles carried in fives. The resin-streaked, narrow, crescent-shaped cones are a feature as they sometimes attain a great length, bunches of up to 45 cm (18 in) are sometimes seen.

P. balfouriana Foxtail pine
ZONE 5

A small tree rare in the wild and in cultivation. Similar in appearance to *P. aristata* but with the foliage carried in more open bundles. It is a native of mountains in the North Coast Range and Sierra Nevada, USA.

P. banksiana   Jack pine or Bank's pine   ZONE 3

A very hardy species from the northern USA and Canada where it grows variably from 7 to 20 m (up to 65 ft) according to the locality. A lime-free soil is suggested and although not particularly ornamental it is a tree valued for its drought-resisting qualities. The pale green leaves are twisted in pairs. Branchlets long and flexible; cones small, remaining closed for many years.

P. bungeana   Lace-bark pine ZONE 4

This Chinese tree can grow to 20 m (over 60 ft) or more, sometimes has several trunks and eventually develops a rounded crown. The main interest lies in the remarkable bark which on a young plant flakes like a Plane tree to reveal the white skin beneath. In older trees the trunk is completely white but one may have to wait a great many years before the effect is seen. Foliage is smooth, dark green; the oval cones are in pairs.

P. canariensis   Canary Island pine   ZONE 7

A tall tree to 30 m or more (over 100 ft) in its natural habitat, where it was once a plentiful forest tree but becoming scarce as stands are reduced. In cultivation in mild areas it makes an attractive small tree with straight trunk, slender lower branches, smooth branchlets and leaves in threes in drooping clusters. Tolerant to lime and a useful tub plant.

P. cembra   Arolla pine   ZONE 4

An alpine species from central Europe and northern Asia with a neat conical or columnar shape. Long lived and slow growing, the plant has downy orange shoots, crowded, rich green leaves in fives; cones erect on the branchlets, purple at first, do not open on the tree but decompose on the ground to release the seeds.

P. cembroides

— — var *cembroides*   Mexican nut pine   ZONE 4

A small tree or large bush usually rather less than 10 m (under 30 ft); from the cooler parts of Mexico and southern Arizona. In growth it is dense with a rounded crown, smooth branchlets, small dark geen leaves in threes or fives curving forward.

— — var *edulis*   Two-leaved nut pine   ZONE 4
In this form the crown is very broad with branches to the ground, leaves are stiff, dark green, small rounded cones very numerous. The edible seeds are marketed as piñones. 'Globe' (Pl. 88) is a small grower with tufts of glaucous needles.

P. contorta

— — var *contorta*   Beach pine or
Shore pine   ZONE 5

Variable from a large bush in the
wild to a tree of some 10 m or
more (over 30 ft) in cultivation.
It is bushy in growth with horizontal branches, shoots slender,
green then greyish, leaves in pairs,
twisted, yellowish-green. A useful
species for dry sandy soils but not
chalk.

— — var *latifolia*   Lodgepole
pine   ZONE 5

A tall tree to 25 m (80 ft) with
broad, straight leaves. Extensively
used for forestry on dry stony
soil. The common name comes
from the American Indians' use as
a centre pole for their lodges.

P. densiflora   Japanese red pine
ZONE 4

A tall-growing Japanese tree
which in many respects is similar
to the Scots pine both in its
mature appearance and reddish
bark, particularly noticeable on a
young plant. On a mature specimen the trunk is nearly always
twisted and inclined, being clear
of branches over much of its
height. The paired leaves which
end in a sharp point are bright
green and the cones, pink-brown,
last for several seasons.

— — 'Oculis-draconis'   Dragon
eye

In this form the leaves are banded

with yellow to give a variegated
effect when viewed from above.

— — 'Pendula'

Usually a low shrub with drooping branches spreading over the
ground.

— — 'Pumila'   Pl. 93

A small growing form.

— — 'Umbraculifera'

A large bush with an umbrella-
like mass of branches, very slow
growing.

P. halepensis   Aleppo pine   ZONE
7

This is a tree of moderate height
up to 20 m (usually under 60 ft),
a native of and much planted in
the Mediterranean area. The
trunk is frequently twisted,
branches irregular, thin smooth
branchlets, with paired green
leaves often tufted towards the
end of branches. These are useful
plants for warm, dry areas in any
well-drained soil. Young plants
are tender but gradually become
more hardy as they develop.

× *holfordiana*   Holford's pine
ZONE 7

With wide-spreading branches
this fast-growing ornamental is a
natural hybrid between the
species *ayacahuite* and *wallichiana*. This hybrid occurred in the
Westonbirt Arboretum, Gloucestershire in 1906 and its name
commemorates the former owner

Sir George Holford. Much like the Bhutan pine in general appearance, with long silver-green leaves and very long narrow cones.

P. jeffreyi Jeffrey's pine ZONE 5

A hardy, highly ornamental tall tree which can get to 60 m (200 ft). A native of the south-west USA, it has bluish leaves in threes on stout shoots. The crown is pyramidal or spire-like on an old tree with a heavy red-brown trunk. Cones are narrow, very long.

P. leucodermis Bosnian pine
ZONE 5

A variable tree to 20 m or more (up to 80 ft) which is a native of Italy and the Balkans. Growth is strong, pyramidal, trunk with grey bark. Paired leaves are stiff, deep glossy green, paler when young and curving inward towards the shoot. The cones are blue at first before becoming brown.

—— 'Compact Gem' Pl. 91
A most attractive, slow growing, dense upright bush with long erect needles heavily clustered in whorls about the stiff shoots.

P. montezumae Pl. 95 Monte-zuma pine ZONE 7

A beautiful tree from the mountains of Mexico and Guatamala with highly decorative leaves. The trunk is reddish-brown and the branches form a large-domed crown. Needles are glaucous green, carried in clusters of from five to eight in upswept tufts. Cones are variable in length. Rather frost tender in cold countries but makes an attractive addition to a cool greenhouse.

P. monticola Western white pine
ZONE 5

An elegant forest tree from western North America. It forms a slender pyramid the thick branches almost hidden by the greyish leaves in clusters of 5. Very long curved cones, pale brown.

P. mugo Pl. 101 Mountain pine
ZONE 2

Variable from low bushy shrubs to trees. Native to the mountains of central Europe these are usually divided by botanists into three groups which differ in their cones. They are very hardy and lime tolerant with stiff, dark green leaves in pairs; prolific flowering, cones carried singly or in clusters.

—— 'Gnome' Pl. 90
A many-branched, dense rounded bush. The radially arranged leaves are dark green carried on yellow-ish shoots. A useful garden plant which eventually reaches 2 m (6 ft 6 in) which was raised from seed of var *mugo* and distributed by Messrs H. den Ouden & Sons of Boskoop, Netherlands.

—— 'Mops' Pl. 94
A superior rock garden subject with short needles forming a low mound.

—— var *mugo* Mugho pine
A broad shrub or occasionally a small tree native from the eastern Alps to the Balkans. Suitable as a background plant in the rock or heather garden.

—— var *pumilio* Pl. 89 Dwarf mountain pine
Also variable but with a large proportion of tiny, dense, almost prostrate shrubs with no definite leader.

P. muricata Pl. 100 Bishop pine ZONE 7

Usually a small tree with flat crown, but sometimes taller and pyramidal. Leaves are in pairs, stiff and twisted; the prolific hooked cones on young plants remain unopened for a great many years often surviving forest fires. They are found in bleak, exposed sea-coast localities in California and are therefore suited to similar situations elsewhere.

P. nigra Pl. 89

Trees with a wide distribution in central and southern Europe. Pyramidal when young becoming domed as they age. When planted in groups they lose their lower branches to reveal the rough, grey-brown trunk. Paired leaves are stiff, bright or dark green.

—— var *caramanica* Crimean pine ZONE 4
A large tree to 30 m (up 100 ft) in cultivation and a native of the Balkans. The trunk is usually divided into several main branches, forming a broad crown.

—— var *cebennensis* Pyrenean pine ZONE 4
Rather lower ultimate height than the above, with long, slender leaves and drooping branches.

—— 'Hornibrookiana' Pl. 96
A shrubby, low grower for the rock garden which was developed from a 'Witches broom' on a wild plant.

—— var *maritima* syn *P. laricio* Corsican pine ZONE 4
This is a common large tree, valued for timber and one of the finest for shelter belts in any soil or situation.

—— var *nigra* syn *P. austriaca* Austrian pine ZONE 4
Rather coarser appearance than the above and also frequently planted. It is a robust grower in virtually any soil; very hardy and dense.

—— 'Pygmaea'
An alpine conifer, very dense, rounded or procumbent with mop-headed branches on old specimens.

P. parviflora Japanese white pine ZONE 5

A tall tree in Japan, much smaller

in cultivation and a favourite subject for training to bonsai form. Immature specimens are conical but become open and flat-topped as they age. Leaves are in fives blue-green paler beneath. A useful ornamental which does best in moist acid soil.

— — 'Adcock's Dwarf'
A slow growing, very compact edition which appeared in Messrs Hilliers Nursery, Ampfield, Romsey, Hampshire. It was named after their propagator, Graham Adcock.

— — 'Glauca'   Pl. 87
A rare variant with conspicuously blue-grey needles.

— — 'Tempelhof'
A seed raised plant which is a faster grower than the type and often develops a stout trunk.

P. patula   Jelecote pine or
Spreading-leaf pine   ZONE 9

An elegant Mexican tree attaining 20 m (65 ft) in mild localities only. Habit is broad and spreading with upswept branches. Leaves very long, held in threes, bright green, in clusters on drooping shoots.

P. peuce   Macedonian pine
ZONE 4

A hardy, disease resistant species with forestry possibilities. Habit is upright, columnar, leaves in fives, blue-green, pale beneath. This species which comes from the Balkans is variable in the wild depending on the altitude.

P. pinaster   Maritime pine or
Cluster pine   ZONE 7

A large tree from the western Mediterranean with a straight trunk, branches in whorls and leaves in pairs. It develops a rounded crown and thrives in light, sandy soils. The large cones are light shiny brown and are sometimes used as ornaments as they do not open as soon as ripe, remaining on the branches for many years. This is the species much planted in the Landes area of south-west France to fix the sand. These have proved a valuable source of resin.

P. pinea   Stone pine or Umbrella
pine   ZONE 9

A familiar plant of the Mediterranean countries unmistakable on account of their picturesque shape of straight trunk and domed crown. Leaves are in pairs, twisted; cones small remaining closed for three or more seasons.

P. ponderosa   Western yellow
pine   ZONE 5

A vigorous, very beautiful tall tree from western North America. Conical when young then variable, usually with bare trunk and few branches. The long needles are in threes carried in tufts at the ends of the stout shoots. Quick growing in any well-drained soil.

P. pumila Dwarf Siberian pine ZONE 3

A variable species from Japan and eastern Asia it is found in exposed mountain sites. Branches are crowded, short, greyish-brown, leaves green with blue-white inner faces. It is sometimes regarded as a geographical race of *P. cembra* as it is similar in many respects, but generally less tall, plants seldom exceeding 3m (10 ft) in height. It is used as a feature plant on a large rockery.

— — 'Glauca'
A selection with blue-grey leaves and tight, compact growth.

P. radiata syn *P. insignis* Monterey pine ZONE 7

A beautiful ornamental tree growing to 30 m (100 ft) with a wide-spreading domed crown. Pyramidal when young with the long branches sweeping the ground. Leaves in threes, bright green, slender on grey shoots. Valued for exposed sea coast sites but subject to frost injury inland due to an early start to the growing season. Rapid growing in New Zealand where it is now an established forest tree.

— — 'Aurea'
A remarkable New Zealand-raised form with light golden-yellow leaves.

P. strobus Eastern white pine or Weymouth pine ZONE 3

A large tree 50 m or more (over 150 ft) from eastern North America. Young trees are conical with smooth grey bark, older specimens develop with large rounded crown. Leaves are in fives, dark blue-green, rather thin; cones are resinous, narrow-cylindrical. Long cultivated as an ornamental and forest tree in Europe where it is rapid growing as a young plant in moist loamy soil.

— — 'Nana'
A group name for several very similar small-growing plants with smaller leaves than the type crowded on dense shoots. These are excellent for the larger rock garden or as specimens in tubs.

P. sylvestris Scots pine ZONE 2

This familiar pine is the dominant forest species which occurs over most of Europe eastwards to Siberia; it is the only native British member of the family. Several geographical variations are known, one growing much taller than the common tree. Young plants are pyramidal then later losing their lower branches to expose the bright orange-red of the trunk. Paired leaves are blue-green, stiff, twisted. A fine plant for dry soils or areas of low rainfall.

—— 'Argentea Compacta' Pl. 92
The name given to a low-growing
bush with silvery needles.

—— 'Aurea'   Pl. 98
New leaves are light yellow-
green, becoming pale green in the
summer and then turning rich
yellow in the winter. Slow growing, rather weak growth, but a
beautiful contrasting colour in the
winter heather garden.

—— 'Beuvronensis'
An outstanding dwarf compact
plant raised in France at the end
of the 19th century. It develops
into a rounded, densely-branched
shrub, at home in the rock garden
or in a large container. Our specimen is less than 0·5 m (18 in) at
fourteen years.

—— 'Fastigiata'
This clone forms an extremely
narrow column with ascending
branches clad with normal grey-
blue leaves.

—— 'Globosa Viridis'
A dwarf globular shrub with
crowded branches and short
branchlets thick with short, stiff
needles.

—— 'Doone Valley'
Another dwarf, rather conical in
shape, with distinctly glaucous
leaves.

—— 'Nana'
A dense dwarf form sometimes
confused with 'Beuvronensis' but
often smaller ultimate size.

—— 'Watereri' syn 'Pumila' Pl. 97
Conical when young becoming
rounded with age: this is not a
dwarf but very slow growing and
could form a useful feature in the
smaller garden.

P. wallichiana   Bhutan pine
ZONE 5

This is a highly ornamental tree of
variable ultimate height up to 40
m (135 ft). A native of the Himalayas where it is found at altitudes of up to 4000 m (13,000 ft).
The long blue-green needles are
in fives, these are normally in
drooping bunches. Cones long,
cylindrical and resinous, erect at
first then hang. Although hardy,
this tree suffers damage from
gales—a point to be remembered
when siting.

Pseudolarix

A monotypic genus containing a single, hardy, deciduous species.
Except for the more wide spreading, level branch system and some
foliage details, this highly ornamental Chinese tree resembles the
larches in general appearance. In gardens they are grown largely on
account of the very attractive autumn coloration of their foliage, the

green leaves turning first to clear yellow then finally rusty-brown before falling. The male flowers are in bunches on short spurs, the females on separate branches on the same tree. Small green cones ripen during the autumn and break up while still on the tree. Well-drained stony or light soil is preferred and where given space, they develop into fine specimens. Frost pockets must be avoided as spring growth, starting early, is sometimes killed back. New plants can be raised by sowing seed in a sheltered position outside during the spring.

P. amabilis   Golden larch   ZONE 5

The single species from eastern China.

Pseudotsuga

The Douglas firs are a group of evergreen trees from North America, China and Japan and although relatively few in species, the Oregon Douglas is one species of considerable economic importance. Except for its excellent but very rare dwarf forms, this species and most of the others are ultimately too large for many gardens—except that they are tolerant of a wide range of soils (excluding chalk), grow rapidly and have dense foliage and so they can be used to advantage to form a quick screen. The long narrow foliage suggests affinity to the Silver firs being soft to the touch and fragrant when squeezed. The small pendulous cones mature the first year and, after releasing their seeds, fall to the ground while still intact. New stock is provided by sowing seed out-of-doors in the spring and transplanting the seedlings at the end of their second year. Cvs have to be grafted.

P. menziesii   Douglas fir   ZONE 6

A well-known, important forest tree which attains great heights in its native western North America and other countries where planting is taking place for timber yield. Because of their speed of growth, one of the main garden uses is for a quick screen—perhaps to hide an ugly building from view. Numerous cvs are on record but these seem to be now either extremely rare or non-existent.

—— var *caesia*   Grey Douglas fir

A variation of the type, slower growing with greyish leaves. Said to be more tolerant of alkaline soils.

—— 'Fletcheri'   Pl. 99

This valuable small edition of the tall tree was discovered in a batch of seedlings in a Surrey, England nursery in 1906. It forms a shrubby bush of irregular outline, with soft radially arranged green leaves, distinctly glaucous blue beneath.

Sciadopitys

This genus contains a single unique tree of considerable garden interest. A very rare plant of central Japan where it is confined to two small areas, but also frequently planted in that country in parks and gardens. Old specimens in time grow into large, upright, usually single trunk trees although as they are slow growing they can be used in small gardens in spite of their eventual size. The foliage consists of two very distinct types of leaves: true leaves are small, yellowish-green, scale-like, appearing with the new growth. The more noticeable false leaves are cladodes, each is composed of two needle-like leaves joined at their edges and appearing as one. Produced in whorls they are deep shining green in a healthy specimen with a yellow line beneath. The whorled clusters of cladodes bear a marked resemblance to the ribs of an inverted umbrella which suggested the former name Parasol pine and today's—the Umbrella pine. Yellow male flowers are in small terminal bunches, females on the same tree develop into attractive, almost round cones which turn brown as they mature during their second year. New plants are raised from seed sown in pots under glass. Young plants should also be protected for at least their first winter by growing on under cover.

S. verticillata   Pl. 102
   Umbrella pine   ZONE 5

The single species.

Tsuga

The Hemlock spruces are a race of evergreen trees with upright trunks, either single or multiple, and generally elegant drooping branches. Some species are fast growing in their native home and valued for the timber produced. *Tsugas* are also highly regarded garden plants for where space permits, the species develop into attractive specimens or an elegant screen. Among the many cvs of *T. canadensis* there are small growers available for the tiniest place. Where growing well there are few finer evergreen trees, the best developing in deep moist loam and showing a preference for acid rather than alkaline conditions. Their linear leaves, glossy green or glaucous with silver reverse, are thickly set, springing spirally from the shoot but usually appearing as if in two opposite rows. Unlike similar arrangements where the leaf tips lie parallel, in *Tsuga* they are uneven for the individual leaves are unequal in length. Except for *T. mertensiana* which has sessile, clustered cones, the mostly small cones are pendulous, ripening the first season but not releasing their winged seeds until the second. The species are increased by sowing seeds in a prepared bed outside during the spring; choice sorts under glass in winter, or cuttings of ripe shoots placed in sandy compost under a light during the autumn. All cvs are propagated by cuttings or layers.

T. canadensis Eastern hemlock
  or Canadian hemlock ZONE 4

A very tall, usually broadly pyramidal tree with a slender trunk usually forked near the base. Horticulturally, the type species does not have quite the same appeal as the very graceful Western hemlock, it has, however, been the source of a range of valuable garden plants especially in the dwarf or slow-growing group. Many of these are available only in North America or rarely from specialists elsewhere. Some of the more easily obtained kinds are listed below.

— — 'Aurea' Golden Canadian
  hemlock
A rare, slow-growing plant of compact, upright form with pale golden-yellow new leaves that fade to yellow-green by summer.

— — 'Bennett' Pl. 106
This is a compact, dense twiggy shrub with its horizontal branches spreading fan-like, eventually forming a low mound. An American-raised plant.

— — 'Cole'
Completely prostrate with long spreading branches, side shoots also trail—the whole forming a dense mat. Can be shaped into a low, weeping plant if stem-trained in its formative years.

— — 'Jeddeloh' Pl. 107
An attractive clone which was raised in Germany and is now proving popular in many countries. The pale green leaves are

carried on slender stems on a compact, very dense, low bushlet.

—— 'Minima'
A slow-growing, ultimately wide-spreading, low bush with dense, rather stiff, flattened branchlets that droop gracefully.

—— 'Pendula' Pl. 105
This is a mound-forming plant. Low for many years the distinctly weeping branches are an arresting sight the year-round but never more than when clad in the new leaves each spring. The photograph on Pl. 105 shows an old specimen on the rock garden at Wisley.

T. caroliniana Carolina hemlock
ZONE 5

A tree which grows to 20 m (65 ft) in the south-eastern USA where it occurs as a mountain plant. In cultivation in Europe it is generally a large bush. Attractive as a specimen with dense growth, reddish or grey young shoots bearing sparse, narrow, dark green leaves with white bands beneath.

T. heterophylla
Western hemlock ZONE 6

The largest of the Hemlock spruces which develops into a tall tree of pyramidal form. The straight trunk has spreading branches with branchlets bearing dark green leaflets each with two broad white bands beneath. With their drooping branch ends and leaders where space and soil conditions permit there are few more elegant trees. They withstand clipping well so may be used to grow a tall hedge. For forestry purposes they are frequently planted beneath deciduous trees in woodland as they are particularly shade tolerant. One of the main dislikes is a chalky soil where plants soon develop a sickly colour.

T. mertensiana Mountain hemlock ZONE 5

Slow-growing and bushy when young, this interesting species from mountain areas of western North America gets very tall, spire-like with age. The forward facing radially set leaves are often silvery or glaucous. Named clones of seedlings which appear as colour variants are named 'Argentea' (Pl. 103) with silver leaves and 'Glauca', a dense slower-growing plant with striking glaucous-blue leaves. The latter is sometimes offered as a grafted plant, *T. canadensis* being used as an understock.

PODOCARPACEAE   Podocarpus family

Dacrydium

A group of about twenty evergreen conifers from South-East Asia and other countries of the South Pacific area. The best species for horticultural use are natives of New Zealand and Tasmania. Varying from large forest trees to tiny alpines all need a warm climate in which to thrive. The foliage is of two distinct types: soft, awl-shaped juvenile and hard, scale-like adult usually present at the same time. The plants are mostly dioecious with the two sexes present on separate trees. The nut-like seeds are held singly in a fleshy (edible) cup. Propagation can be from seed although in practice young specimens are gathered from the wild when small and grown-on in containers until large enough to plant out. The alpine species will root from cuttings or layered.

D. cupressinum   Pl. 110   Rimu
ZONE 9

Although wild trees attain a great height, the species is slow growing if away from its native habitat and makes a fine garden ornamental. The semi-pendulous branchlets of cypress-like foliage often take on a reddish hue in cold weather. Formerly the principal timber tree of New Zealand, but now becoming more scarce as stands are reduced. The heavy wood, known as red pine, has many applications in the building trade.

D. laxifolium   Pygmy pine
ZONE 7

A prostrate, eventually mat-forming species with long, thin branches clad with tiny adult leaves, generally green or blue in colour and which become a rich purple in winter.

D. franklinii   Huon pine   ZONE 9

A tall pyramidal evergreen in its native Tasmania, this is generally a large bush when cultivated in other countries. It has thin, graceful, weeping branches bearing bright green scale-like leaves.

Phyllocladus

An interesting group of conifers with unusual evergreen foliage. Almost all are native to New Zealand and Tasmania and only one, *P. alpinus*, can be considered hardy enough to plant outside in Britain. The plants of this genus have a completely different appearance from other conifers due to the fact that in the adult foliage stage the leaves are represented by cladodes or flattened leaf-like branchlets which function both as stem and leaf, the true or original leaves are tiny, scale-like. The flowers of each sex can be found either on a single tree or on individuals according to species. After fertilisation, the tiny nut-like seeds appear in clusters at the base of the growing shoots. Deep, rich soil is suggested in order to produce good specimens, this is in mild areas only. Propagation is from seed or cuttings under glass in the autumn, the latter often root better during the spring.

P. alpinus Mountain toa-toa
ZONE 7

A curious shrubby plant of irregular outline with flattened green 'leaves'. Its tiny bright red male flowers speckle the plant during the spring. For a sheltered rock garden.

P. tricomanoides Celery pine or Tanekaha ZONE 9

A tall tree reaching 23 m (75 ft) in its native New Zealand. The flattened modified branchlets (cladodes), although smaller, resemble thick celery leaves in shape.

Podocarpus

A large genus of mostly evergreen shrubs and trees. The few hardy species are variable in appearance, some slow growing and suitable for small gardens, others although eventually tall forest trees in their homeland are ornamental subjects when young; at least one species will make a good dense hedge. The foliage is thick, often hard and pointed, spirally arranged on the shoots. Flowers are normally present on separate plants. The colourful fruits are an added attraction when ripe with the single hard seed embedded in the end of a fleshy coloured stalk. Podocarps will grow in most soils including lime or chalk. Propagation can be carried out in late summer using firm wood to make cuttings, which should be placed under glass to root.

P. acutifolius Pl. 113 ZONE 7

Commonly treated as a shrub in gardens, although in New Zea-

land it grows into a small tree of 10 m (33 ft) or more. The olive-green prickly leaves have suggested that it could be used as a hedge plant both in its homeland and in Britain although usually treated as a rockery subject in the latter country.

P. alpinus ZONE 7

Dense, hardy, low bush thickly clad with dark green yew-like leaves. An interesting rockery subject from Australia.

P. andinus Plum-fruited yew
ZONE 7

Usually seen as a many-stemmed tall bush, this species from the Chilean Andes has soft, dark green leaves sometimes twisted on the branchlets to reveal two pale bands beneath. Sometimes seen are the oval black fruits.

P. dacrydioides White pine
ZONE 9

A graceful tree attaining up to 50 m (160 ft) and on a mature specimen frequently clear of branches for nearly half its height. The long weeping branches bear short bronze-green leaves arranged spirally on the shoots. Flowering takes place in the spring, and when later the young seeds are developing, they are bright blue and held in a red aril.

P. ferrugineus Brown pine
ZONE 9

A tall New Zealand tree with its trunk clad in grey-brown bark.

The pale green yew-like leaves are arranged irregularly in two opposite rows on the branchlets. The bloomed red fruits (drupes) appear in winter.

P. nivalis Alpine totara ZONE 6

A low bush-like species from New Zealand with dense branches clad with small, leathery, pale green leaves.

P. salignus Willow podocarp
ZONE 7

Large, open-branched shrub or small tree with long, dark green, willow-like leaves which are pale beneath. A native of Chile sometimes seen planted outside in mild parts of southern Britain where it forms a conical-shaped bush.

P. spicatus Black pine ZONE 8

A choice half-hardy New Zealand species of delicate appearance with its slender branchlets bearing small, greenish-bronze leaflets.

P. totara Totara ZONE 8

Another of those species which reaches large timber-tree proportions in New Zealand. The wood being durable it finds many uses in the building trade and also for fencing. As a young tree it is a fine ornamental with small, yellow-green, rather prickly leaves.

— — 'Aurea' Pl. 114 Golden
totara
This superb golden-leaved ver-
sion makes a striking specimen for those prepared to wait as growth tends to be slow in its early years.

TAXODIACAE   Swamp Cypress family

Athrotaxis

Tasmanian cedars are a small genus of interest. They are evergreen with pendulous branches and, as their common name suggests, they are natives of Tasmania. In their natural habitat growth is tall, in cooler climates they are slow to attain much size and are best classed as tall shrubs. Their foliage is small, awl-shaped, overlapping, surrounding the shoot. The cones are similar in structure to a near relation—the Swamp cypress, being spiny with many overlapping scales. The best plants are usually seen growing in moist acid soil. New stock can be raised from seed but as these are generally hard to come by most plants offered for sale are grown from small cuttings placed in sandy compost in a greenhouse during the late summer. Alternatively, they could be grafted using *Cryptomeria japonica* as understocks. This would be under glass during the spring.

A. cupressoides ZONE 8

This graceful, small tree in the wild becomes more shrub-like when grown in cooler parts of the world. Recalling a whipcord *Hebe* in form, the branches are clothed with small, dark green leaves pressed tightly to the stem.

A. laxifolia ZONE 7

Like its close relative above this too is moderately hardy in the milder parts of southern Britain and Ireland. It differs in its greater ultimate height and larger, more open, spiny tipped leaves.

A. selaginoides King William pine ZONE 9

More tender than the two species already mentioned this has large, leathery, *Cryptomeria*-like leaves which are carried on stout branchlets. At one time in prehistory, a very similar plant formed part of the indigenous flora of south-east England.

Cryptomeria

A genus comprising of a single, distinctive species. A native of Japan and China it has also been planted in these countries since early times to provide a valuable source of timber. In deep, rich soil, well provided with moisture some very large specimens of over 50 m (over 150 ft) have been recorded. The type species when cultivated in Europe is rarely half of that height and small trees or large bushes are more usual. When choosing a site for planting, remember that a position sheltered from the cold wind will suit them best. As with most of the other evergreen conifers, the difference between juvenile and adult foliage is considerable; the former, open, awl-shaped and soft to touch is retained in some cvs. Others carry a mixture of this and the smaller hard, adult type. A few are adult only. The foliage colour varies from the typical light green of the summer months to reddish-bronze or dull brown in autumn and winter. The flowers of the two sexes are carried on the same tree; males in terminal clusters, females on separate branchlets. Round cones are green at first and brown when ripe. Although the type can be raised from seed, all the others are cvs and as such have to be grown from cuttings. These root with ease if placed in light compost, under glass during the summer.

C. japonica Pl. 115 Japanese cedar ZONE 5

The single species from Japan and China represented in cultivation in the West by the var *sinensis*.

— — 'Bandai-sugi' Pl. 118
This charming, very dense, rounded dwarf is composed of stiff irregular shoots of congested green leaves which turn reddish in winter.

— — 'Compressa' Pl. 116
A rounded bushlet of thick branchlets bearing tiny, densely arranged juvenile leaves, deep green in summer, reddish-brown in winter.

— — 'Cristata' Pl. 111
Large rather open bush made up of thick ascending branches some of which have their ends flattened (fasciated) into large cockscomb-like growths.

— — 'Elegans'
A popular, most attractive fixed juvenile foliage form, its soft billowy masses of green leaves changes in colour as the season advances, first to red then bronze during the cold of winter. It is an upright grower and eventually a small tree.

— — 'Elegans Aurea'
Similar foliage arrangement to the above but with yellow new shoots and pale yellow-green leaves, glaucous on the reverse. Less tall than 'Elegans' its colour is held the year-round.

— — 'Elegans Compacta'
Variable—generally more compact than the others of this type and although the name suggests a dwarf, this is seldom so, the plant developing into a wide, floppy bush. The individual leaves are soft, needle-like. 'Plumosa' is yet another form available in New Zealand, much like 'Elegans' but with brighter green leaves.

— — 'Globosa' Pl. 117
Rounded, very dense bush form composed of pendulous shoots with bright-green leaves. 'Bandai-sugi' (Pl. 118) is much more compact with its closely-set leaves on much reduced shoots. One of the choicest of all rock garden conifers.

— — 'Jindai-sugi'
Another dense, low grower. Raised in Japan, it has both erect and spreading branches and forms an irregular flat-topped bush of bright green leaves.

— — 'Lobbii'
Tall erect tree of columnar form with short branches and long branchlets often crowded into bunches. The foliage arrangement is distinct with the small bright green leaves pointing forward along the shoots.

— — 'Monstrosa'
An irregular-branched pyramidal bush with many clustered branchlets some thickened with congested foliage at the tips.

— — 'Nana' ('Elegans Nana') ('Lobbii Nana')
Compact, rounded bush of slender branchlets, pendulous at the tips. Light green leaves of differing lengths, long on the main branches, tiny on the ultimate shoots, which in winter are thickened with clusters of male flowers.

— — 'Spiralis'
Unmistakable, with rather thick, bright green leaves twisted spirally around the thin branchlets. The typical plant seen is an unevenly rounded bush although old tall trees are known, possibly the result of grafting early plants on to a vigorous stock.

— — 'Sekkan-sugi' Pl. 112
A newcomer with light golden-cream foliage. It appears to be quick growing and uneven bush-like in form.

— — 'Spiraliter Falcata'
This displays a similar foliage arrangement to 'Spiralis', but with the green, smaller leaves of irregular size carried on long, twisting branches to form an open, tall bush.

— — 'Vilmoriniana'
Apart from 'Compressa' this cv can be confused with no other. It grows into a ball of dense branchlets clad with tiny, recurved, light green leaves which turn brownish in winter.

— — 'Viminalis'
This with its very long, slender green whipcord-like branches develops into an open, often straggling, bush with many of the branchlets gathered into terminal bunches.

Metasequoia

This genus contains a single living species, which was discovered in Hupeh Province, China as recently as 1941. Living specimens raised from collected seed were introduced a few years later. Like *Ginkgo*, these plants are also known as fossil remains and before the discovery of the living material, they were thought to be long extinct. Deciduous, and recalling the Swamp cypress in form, this also shows an affinity for water and the best specimens are seen where the soil remains moist in hot weather. The trunk, which in later life becomes deeply fissured, is covered in red-brown bark. Branches are upswept and form a pyramidal-shape. Foliage is fresh green changing to rust-red before being shed in the autumn. The cones are carried on the ends of long leafy stalks and ripen in their first season. Propagation is from either seeds or cuttings placed in sandy compost under glass during the late summer.

M. glytostroboides Dawn redwood ZONE 5

The single species from China, ultimately to 30 m (100 ft).

Sequoia

Tall, noble evergreen trees found in the wild only along the Pacific seaboard of the USA. The genus contains a single species which has among its numbers the world's tallest tree. Plants are narrowly pyramidal in outline with whorled branches, old trees retaining lower branches only when grown in isolation. Even here, much of the basal part is bare but usually with thickets of branchlets springing directly from the trunk. Under natural forest conditions they develop tall, straight trunks covered in thick reddish bark and often devoid of branches over much of their height. The dark green, abruptly pointed, linear leaves, recalling those of the yew, are in two rows on the side branchlets; on the leading shoots they are smaller, radial, clasping the stem. Damage to leaves by frost and wind does not appear to restrict growth although it is unsightly and is a point to be borne in mind when selecting a site for the two splendid cvs mentioned below. The flowers of the two sexes are on the same tree, the females forming small rounded cones which ripen in two seasons and remain on the tree for several years. New plants can be raised from seed. The cvs from cuttings or layers. Young plants usually require protection through their first winter.

S. sempervirens Californian redwood or Coast redwood ZONE 7

The single species from California and Oregon.

—— 'Adpressa' Pl. 109
A beautiful dwarf shrub with grey leaves and creamy-white tips to the new shoots. Left to itself the plant invariably develops a leader and unless this erect growth is removed, the plant grows into a tall tree. Should a specimen outgrow its place it may be cut right back with safety, new shoots springing from the bole.

—— 'Prostrata' Pl. 108
An attractive form with grey leaves twice the width of the type. Sometimes completely prostrate, it can be encouraged to form a mound by tidying the branch ends. Occasionally this plant will throw up a strong leader which will take over and develop into a small tree.

Sequoiadendron

Giant trees allied to *Sequoia*, from which they differ mainly in their scale-like leaves. They do not attain such great height as the other redwood or large Douglas firs but are massive in girth and live to a great age. Some of the specimens seen in Britain—where they are planted in parks and large gardens, or perhaps as an avenue leading to a great mansion—are the original seedlings sent out by the nursery firm of Veitch of Exeter. These seedlings were raised from seed obtained by their collector William Lobb in 1853. Individual leaves are tiny, carried thickly on slender shoots which hang in great bunches on the side branches. The red-brown bark is a feature on trees of all ages, it gets extremely thick in time and—as small boys will know—can be punched hard without hurting the fist. Cones, larger than those of *Sequoia*, ripen in their second year. The seeds produced will increase the type, cvs grow from cuttings of the current year's wood or grafting, under glass, in late summer.

S. giganteum Wellingtonia
ZONE 6

The single species from California.

—— 'Pendulum' Weeping sequoia

One specimen of this rare and unique conifer can have long drooping branches, seemingly weighted down with heavy foliage. Another grows into a tall tree with short erect branches held close to the trunk and pendulous branchlets of dark green leaves.

—— 'Pygmaeum'

Compact, dense bush of triangular outline with leaves more glaucous than the type. Although a smaller edition of the giant tree, it is hardly a dwarf.

Taxodium

Hardy, tall, deciduous trees with attractive foliage from the USA and Mexico. Apart from very dry soils (which are best avoided) they thrive in most sites, including really wet places such as pond sides. The tree comes into leaf very late in Britain—one of the last to do so. The leaves have a delicate feathery appearance, pale green at first. Shoots are of two kinds: the leading shoots in which the leaves grow spirally are retained, and the side branchlets where the leaves are carried in opposite rows are deciduous, falling with the now rust-red leaves in the autumn. The round cones are carried on short stalks and ripen the first season. Seed should be sown under glass during the spring; cuttings of firm wood placed in moist soil under a glass light during the autumn will probably have rooted by the spring, but is better if left for another year before transplanting to a nursery bed.

T. ascendens Pond cypress
ZONE 5

This tall, pyramidal tree from the south-east USA bears spreading branches and small erect branchlets with adpressed light green leaves.

—— 'Nutans'

A narrow columnar sort with short ascending branches, and branchlets erect at first then nodding, carrying awl-shaped leaves which are incurved, densely arranged.

T. distichum   Swamp cypress
ZONE 4

Occurring in wet places over much of the southern part of the USA and thriving in similar situations in cultivation. Slow growing but eventually tall, it is an attraction at all stages of growth.

APPENDIX

Check-list of Conifer Families and Genera

GINKGOALES

GINKGOACEAE   Ginkgo family

Ginkgo

TAXALES

TAXACEAE   Yew family

*Amenotaxus**	*Pseudotaxus**
*Austrotaxus**	*Taxus*
Cephalotaxus	*Torreya*

CONIFERALES

ARAUCARIACEAE   Chile pine family

Agathis	*Araucaria*

CUPRESSACEAE   Cypress family

*Actinostrobus**	*Juniperus*
Austrocedrus	*Libocedrus**
Callitris	*Microbiota**
Calocedrus	*Neocallitropsis**
Chamaecyparis	*Papuacedrus**
× *Cupressocyparis*	*Pilgerodendron**
Cupressus	*Tetraclinis**
*Diselma**	*Thuja*
*Fitzroya**	*Thujopsis*
*Fokienia**	*Widdringtonia**

* Members of these genera are not described in the text.

PINACEAE   Pine family

Abies
Cathaya*
Cedrus
Keteleeria*
Larix

Picea
Pinus
Pseudolarix
Pseudotsuga
Tsuga

PODOCARPACEAE   Podocarp family

Acmopyle*
Dacrydium
Microcachrys*
Microstrobos*

Phyllocladus
Podocarpus
Saxe-gothaea*

TAXODIACEAE   Swamp Cypress family

Athrotaxis
Cryptomeria
Cunninghamia*
Glyptostrobus*
Metasequoia

Sciadopitys
Sequoia
Sequoiadendron
Taiwania*
Taxodium

GLOSSARY

Gardening and botanical terms used in the book.

Acid (soil)   Lime-free

Alkaline (soil)   Containing lime or chalk

Apex or apice (plural)   Topmost

Apical buds   *see* Apex

Ascending   Curving upwards

Aril   Fleshy seed holder

Awl-like   A leaf, often slightly curved, tapering from the base to the tip

Axil   The angle between branch and branchlet or branchlet and leaf

Break   To branch; to send out new shoots from dormant wood

Columnar   Narrow cylindrical, column-like

Compost   Mixture of prepared soils used for potting, *see also* Garden compost

Cone   Seed-bearing structure

Conelet   Immature cone

Conical   Cone-shaped

Cultivar   An internationally accepted term for a plant only found in cultivation

Deciduous   Leaf losing in one season or less

Elite   Specimens selected for excellence

Evergreen   Leaves retained the year-round

Fastigiate   Branches upright close together

Fertile flower   Seed-bearing

Garden compost   Correctly rotted down garden refuse

Glaucous   Foliage with a covering of 'bloom', usually grey or bluish

Humus   Powder-like particles in the soil derived from decayed vegetable matter

Lateral   Emerging from the side

Mutate   *see* Sport

Node   Leaf joint; in conifers often the division between two years' growth

Pendulous   Drooping downwards

Plumose   Feathery

Prostrate   Lying flat on the ground

Pyramidal   Broad-based tapering evenly towards the tip

Scale   A minute form of leaf, often adult, sometimes papery and deciduous

Sport   Bud mutation, frequently the source of a new cv

Spur   Short, stiff branchlet

Stomatic   Bands of 'breathing pores' (stoma) on the foliage, usually grey or white

Strike   To root

Strobulus   Cone- or catkin-like arrangement of male and female flowers

Type   The original specimen to be named but usually is taken to mean the normal form of a plant

SELECT BIBLIOGRAPHY

Works of reference used in the compilation of
this book which are suggested for further reading.

Bean, W. J. *Trees and Shrubs hardy in the British Isles* 7th edn. John
Murray, London (1951).

Dahl, M. and Thygesen, T. B. *Garden Pests and Diseases of Flowers
and Shrubs* Blandford Press, London (1974).

Harrison, C. R. *Ornamental Conifers* Reed, Wellington (1975).

Hillier, H. G. *Hilliers' Manual of Trees and Shrubs* revised edn. David
and Charles, Newton Abbott (1975).

den Ouden, P. and Boom, B. K. *Manual of Cultivated Conifers*
Martinus Nijhoff, The Hague (1965).

Mitchell, A. *Trees of Britain and Northern Europe* Collins, London
(1974).

Kiaer, E. and Huxley, A. *Garden Planning and Planting* Blandford
Press, Poole (1976).

Salmon, J. T. *New Zealand Flowers and Plants in Colour* 4th edn.
Reed, Wellington (1974).

Welch, H. J. *Dwarf Conifers* 2nd edn. Faber and Faber, London
(1968).

INDEX OF PLANTS DESCRIBED
Numbers in bold type refer to the colour plates

Abies 163
— *alba* 164
— *amabilis* 164
— — 'Spreading Star' 164
— *balsamea* 164
— — 'Hudsonia' **70**, 164
— *cephalonica* 164
— *concolor* 164
— — 'Candicans' 165
— — 'Compacta' 165
— — 'Glauca Prostrate' **73**, 165
— var *lowiana* 165
— — 'Violacea' 165
— — 'Wattezii' 165
— *delavayi* 165
— var *forresti* 165
— *fargesii* 165
— *grandis* 165
— — 'Aurea' 166
— *homolepis* 166
— *koreana* 166
— *lasiocarpa* 166
— — 'Compacta' **69**, 166
— *magnifica* 166
— — 'Glauca' 166
— *mariesii* 166
— *nordmanniana* 166
— — 'Pendula' 167
— — 'Golden Spreader' 167
— — 'Prostrata' 167
— *numidica* 167
— — 'Pendula' 167
— *pindrow* 167
— — var *brevifolia* 167
— *pinsapo* 167
— — 'Aurea' 167
— — 'Glauca' **71**, 167

— *procera* 168
— — 'Glauca' **72**, 168
— — 'Glauca Prostrate', *see*
    A. procera
— *veitchii* 168

Agathis 126
— *australis* **4** 126

Araucaria 126
— *araucana* 127
— *bidwillii* 127
— *heterophylla* 127

Athrotaxis 196
— *cupressoides* 196
— *laxifolia* 196
— *selaginoides* 196

Austrocedrus 128
— *chilensis* 128

Callitris 128
— *columellaris* 128
— *oblonga* 128
— *rhomboidea* 129

Calocedrus 129
— *decurrens* 129
— — 'Aureovariegata' 129
— — 'Columnaris' 129
— — 'Intricata' 129
— *formosana* 129
— *macrolepis* 129

Cedrus 168
— *atlantica* 169

209

Cedrus atlantica—contd.
— — 'Aurea' 169
— — 'Fastigiata' 169
— — var *glauca* ('Glauca') 169
— — 'Glauca Pendula' 169
— — 'Pendula' 169
— — 'Pyramidalis' 170
— *brevifolia* 170
— *deodara* 170
— — 'Albospica' 170
— — 'Aurea' 170
— — 'Aurea Pendula' **68**, 170
— — 'Pendula' 170
— — 'Pygmy' 170
— — 'Robusta' 170
— *libani* 170
— — 'Comte de Dijon' 171
— — 'Golden Dwarf' 171
— — 'Nana' 171
— — 'Pendula' 171
— — 'Sargentii' 171
— — var *stenocoma* 171

Cephalotaxus 124
— *fortuni* 124
— *harringtonia* 125
— — var *drupacea* 125
— — 'Fastigiata' 125
— — 'Prostrata' 125

Chamaecyparis 130
— *formosensis* 130
— *lawsoniana* 130
— — 'Albospica' 131
— — 'Albovariegata' **21**, 131
— — 'Allumii' 131
— — 'Aurea Densa' 131
— — 'Aureovariegata' 131
— — 'Backhouse Silver', *see*
        'Pygmaea Argentea'
— — 'Blom' 131
— — 'Chilworth Silver', *see*
        'Ellwoodii'
— — 'Columnaris' 131
— — 'Duncanii' **20**, 131
— — 'Ellwoodii' 131

— — 'Ellwood's Gold' **18**, 131
— — 'Ellwood's Pygmy' 131
— — 'Ellwood's White' 131
— — 'Erecta Viridis' 132
— — 'Erecta Filiformis' 132
— — 'Erecta Aurea' 132
— — 'Erecta Alba' 132
— — 'Filiformis' 132
— — 'Filiformis Compacta', *see*
        'Filiformis'
— — 'Filiformis Glauca', *see*
        'Filiformis'
— — 'Fleckellwood', *see* 'Ellwoodii'
— — 'Fletcheri' **15**, 132
— — 'Fletcher's White', *see*
        'Fletcheri'
— — 'Forsteckensis' **13**, 132
— — 'Fraseri' **6**, 132
— — 'Gimbornii' **10**, 133
— — 'Gnome' **8**, 133
— — 'Gold Splash', *see* 'Fletcheri'
— — 'Golden King' 133
— — 'Grayswood Pillar' 133
— — 'Green Globe', *see* 'Gnome'
— — 'Green Hedger' 133
— — 'Green Pillar' 133
— — 'Hillieri' **7**, 133
— — 'Imbricata Pendula' 133
— — 'Intertexta' 133
— — 'Kilmacurragh' 133
— — 'Knowefieldensis' 133
— — 'Kooy' 134
— — 'Lane' 134
— — 'Limelight', *see* 'Silver Queen'
— — 'Lutea' **12**, 134
— — 'Lycopodioides' 134
— — 'Minima' 134
— — 'Minima Aurea' **9**, 134
— — 'Minima Glauca' 134
— — 'Moonlight', *see* 'Silver Queen'
— — 'Nana' 134
— — 'Nidiformis' 134
— — 'Nyewood, *see* 'Chilworth
        Silver'
— — 'Pembury Blue' 134
— — 'Pottenii' 134

Chamaecyparis lawsoniana—contd.
— — 'Pygmaea Argentea' **14**, 134
— — 'Rogersii' 135
— — 'Silver Queen' 135
— — 'Smithii' 135
— — 'Snow Flurry', *see* 'Fletcheri'
— — 'Spek' 135
— — 'Stewartii' 135
— — 'Tamariscifolia' 135
— — 'Tharandtensis Caesia' 135
— — 'Triomf van Boskoop' 135
— — 'Versicolor' 135
— — 'Westermanii' **11**, 135
— — 'Winston Churchill' 135
— — 'Wisselii' 136
— — 'Yellow Transparent', *see*
      'Fletcheri'
— — 'Youngii' 136
— *nootkatensis* 136
— — 'Aurea', *see* 'Lutea'
— — 'Aureovariegata', *see* 'Lutea'
— — 'Argenteovariegata', *see*
      'Lutea'
— — 'Lutea' 136
— — 'Pendula' 136
— — 'Variegata', *see* 'Lutea'
— *obtusa* 136
— — 'Albospica' 137
— — 'Aurea' 137
— — 'Bassett' 137
— — 'Caespitosa' 137
— — 'Chabo-yadori' 137
— — 'Compacta' 137
— — 'Coralliformis' 137
— — 'Crippsii' 137
— — 'Fernspray Gold' **39**, 137
— — 'Filicoides' 138
— — 'Goldspire' 138
— — 'Hage' 138
— — 'Intermedia' 138
— — 'Juniperoides' 138
— — 'Kosteri' **23**, 138
— — 'Lycopodioides' 138
— — 'Lycopodioides Aurea', *see*
      'Lycopodioides'
— — 'Mariesii' 138

— — 'Minima' 138
— — 'Nana' 138
— — 'Nana Aurea' 138
— — 'Nana Gracilis' 139
— — 'Nana Pyramidalis' 139
— — 'Nana Lutea' **24**, 139
— — 'Pygmaea' 139
— — 'Pygmaea Aurescens', *see*
      'Pygmaea'
— — 'Repens' 139
— — 'Rigid Dwarf' 139
— — 'Sanderi' 139
— — 'Spiralis' 139
— — 'Tetragona Aurea' **36**, 140
— *pisifera* 140
— — 'Aurea' 140
— — 'Aurea Nana' 140
— — 'Boulevard' **29**, **31**, 140
— — 'Compacta' **28**, 141
— — 'Compacta Variegata' 141
— — 'Filifera' **25**, 141
— — 'Filifera Aurea' **26**, 141
— — 'Filifera Nana', *see* 'Filifera'
— — 'Golden Mop', *see* 'Filifera
      Aurea'
— — 'Gold Spangle' **29**, 141
— — 'Nana' 141
— — 'Nana Variegata' 141
— — 'Plumosa' 141
— — 'Plumosa Albopicta' 141
— — 'Plumosa Aurea' 142
— — 'Plumosa Aurea Compacta'
      30, 142
— — 'Plumosa Compressa' **34**,
      142
— — 'Plumosa Flavescens' 142
— — 'Plumosa Rogersii' 142
— — 'Snow' **35**, 142
— — 'Squarrosa' **32**, 142
— — 'Squarrosa Dumosa' 142
— — 'Squarrosa Intermedia' **33**,
      142
— — 'Squarrosa Sulphurea' **38**,
      143
— *thyoides* 143
— — 'Andelyensis' 143

Chamaecyparis thyoides—contd.
— — 'Andelyensis Nana', *see*
    'Andelyensis'
— — 'Aurea' 145
— — 'Ericoides' 143
— — 'Glauca' 143
— — 'Variegata' 143

Cryptomeria 197
—*japonica* **115**, 197
— — 'Bandai-sugi' **118**, 197
— — 'Compressa' **116**, 197
— — 'Cristata' **111**, 197
— — 'Elegans' 197
— — 'Elegans Aurea' 198
— — 'Elegans Compacta' 198
— — 'Globosa' **117**, 198
— — 'Jindai-sugi' 198
— — 'Lobbii' 198
— — 'Monstrosa' 198
— — 'Nana' 198
— — 'Spiralis' 198
— — 'Sekkan-sugi' **112**, 198
— — 'Spiraliter Falcata' 198
— — 'Vilmoriniana' 199
— — 'Viminalis' 199

× *Cupressocyparis* 144
—*leylandii* **45**, 144
— — 'Castlewellan' 144
— — 'Green Spire' 144
— — 'Haggerston Grey' 144
— — 'Leighton Green' 144
— — 'Naylor's Blue' 144
— — 'Stapehill' 144

Cupressus 145
—*cashmeriana* 145
—*funebris* 145
—*glabra* 145
— — 'Aurea' 146
— — 'Blue Pyramid', *see*
    'Pyramidalis'
— — 'Hodgins' 146
— — 'Pyramidalis' **41**, 146
— — 'Variegata' **40**, 146

—*lusitanica* 146
— — var *benthami* 146
—*macrocarpa* 146
— — 'Aurea' 147
— — 'Aurea Saligna', *see* 'Conybeari'
— — 'Conybeari' 147
— — 'Donard Gold' 147
— — 'Gold Cone', *see* 'Donard
    Gold'
— — 'Goldcrest', *see* 'Donard
    Gold'
— — 'Golden Pillar', *see* 'Donard
    Gold'
— — 'Horizontalis Aurea' **44**,
    147
—*lambertiana* 'Aurea', *see*
    'Horizontalis Aurea'
— — 'Lutea' 141
—*sempervirens* 147
— — 'Stricta' 147
— — 'Gracilis' 148
— — 'Swane's Golden' **43**, 148
—*torulosa* 148
— — 'Corneyana' 148

Dacrydium 193
—*cupressinum* **110**, 193
—*laxifolium* 193
—*franklinii* 193

Ginkgo 121
—*biloba* 121
— — 'Autumn Gold' 121
— — 'Fastigiata' 121
— — 'Fairmount' 121
— — 'Pendula' 121
— — 'Tremonia' 121

Juniperus 148
—*chinensis* 149
— — 'Aurea' 149
— — 'Japonica' 149
— — 'Kaizuka' 149
— — 'Kaizuka Variegata', *see*
    'Kaizuka'
— — 'Obelisk' **59**, 149

Juniperus chinensis—contd.
—— 'Oblonga' 150
—— 'Pyramidalis' **65**, 150
—— 'San Jose' 150
—— 'Stricta' 150
—— 'Variegata' 150
— *communis* 150
—— 'Compressa' **55**, 150
—— 'Depressa Aurea' **62**, 150
—— 'Depressed Star' 150
—— 'Hibernica' **61**, 150
—— 'Hornibrookii' 151
—— 'Repanda' 151
—— 'Silver Lining' 151
—— 'Suecica' 151
—— 'Suecica Nana', *see* 'Suecica'
—— 'Vase' 151
— *conferta* 151
— *davurica* 151
—— 'Expansa' 151
—— 'Expansa Aureospicata' 151
—— 'Expansa Variegata' 151

— *horizontalis* 152
—— 'Bar Harbor' 152
—— 'Douglasii' 152
—— 'Glauca', *see* 'Wiltonii'
—— 'Montana' 152
—— 'Plumosa' 152
—— 'Wiltonii' 152
— × *media* 152
—— 'Blaauw' 152
—— 'Gold Coast' 153
—— 'Hetzii' **64**, 153
—— 'Old Gold' 153
—— 'Pfitzerana' 153
—— 'Pfitzerana Aurea' **67**, 153
—— 'Pfitzerana Compacta', *see*
        'Pfitzerana'
—— 'Pfitzerana Glauca', *see*
        'Pfitzerana'
—— 'Mint Julep', *see* 'Pfitzerana'
—— 'Plumosa' 153
—— 'Plumosa Aurea' 153
— *procumbens* **57**, 153
—— 'Bonin Isles', *see* 'Nana'

—— 'Nana' 58, 154
— *recurva* 154
—— var *coxii* **66**, 154
—— 'Embley Park' 154
— *rigida* 154
— *sabina* 154
—— 'Arcadia' 155
—— 'Blue Danube' 155
—— 'Erecta', *see sabina*
—— 'Hicksii' 155
—— 'Skandia' 155
—— var *tamariscifolia* **60**, 155
—— 'Variegata' 155
—— 'Von Ehren' 155
— *sargentii* 155
— *scopulorum* 155
—— 'Blue Haven', *see* 'Blue
        Heaven'
—— 'Blue Heaven' 155
—— 'Gray Gleam' 156
—— 'Hillborn's Silver Globe'
        156
—— 'Pathfinder' 156
—— 'Platinum' 156
—— 'Springbank' 156
—— 'Tabletop' 156
— *squamata* 156
—— 'Blue Star' **56**, 156
—— 'Meyeri' 156
—— 'Wilsoni' 156
— *virginiana* 157
—— 'Burkii' 157
—— 'Canaertii' 157
—— 'Grey Owl' **63**, 157
—— 'Schottii' 157
—— 'Skyrocket' 157

Larix 171
— *decidua* 172
—— 'Pendula' 172
— × *eurolepis* 172
— *kaempferi* 172
—— 'Pendula' 173

Metasequoia 199
— *glyptostroboides* 199

Phyllocladus 193
— *alpinus* 194
— *tricomanoides* 194

Picea 173
— *abies* 173
— — 'Acrocona' 174
— — 'Aurea' 174
— — 'Clanbrassiliana' 174
— — 'Cranstonii' 174
— — 'Echiniformis' **82**, 174
— — 'Gregoryana' 174
— — 'Inversa' 174
— — 'Little Gem' **77**, 174
— — 'Nidiformis' **80**, 174
— — 'Ohlendorffii' **76**, 174
— — var *pendula* 174
— — 'Pendula Major' 175
— — 'Procumbens' 175
— — 'Pumila Nigra' 175
— — 'Reflexa' 175
— — 'Remontii' 175
— — 'Repens' 175
— *brewerana* **75**, 175
— *engelmannii* 175
— *glauca* 175
— — var *albertiana* 'Cornica', *see* 'Conica'
— — 'Conica' **81**, 176
— — 'Echiniformis' 176
— — 'Nana' 176
— *jezoensis* 176
— — var *hondoensis* 176
— *likiangensis* 176
— — var *purpurea* 176
— *mariana* 176
— — 'Doumetii' **86**, 177
— — 'Nana' **79**, 177
— *omorika* **84**, 177
— — 'Expansa' 177
— — 'Nana' 177
— — 'Pendula' 177
— *orientalis* 177
— — 'Aurea' **85**, 177
— — 'Gracilis' 178
— *polita* 178

— *pungens* 178
— — 'Compacta' 178
— — 'Glauca' 178
— — 'Glauca Prostrate' **83**, 178
— — 'Endtz' 179
— — 'Globosa' **78**, 179
— — 'Koster' 179
— — 'Moerheimii' 179
— — 'Pendula' 179
— — 'Thomsen' 179
— *sitchensis* 179
— *smithiana* 179

Pinus 180
— *aristata* 181
— *armandii* 181
— *ayacahuite* 181
— *balfouriana* 181
— *banksiana* 182
— *bungeana* 182
— *canariensis* 182
— *cembra* 182
— *cembroides* 182
— — var *edulis* 182
— — 'Globe' 182
— *contorta* 183
— — var *latifolia* 183
— *densiflora* 183
— — 'Oculis-draconis' 183
— — 'Pendula' 183
— — 'Pumila' **93**, 183
— — 'Umbraculifera' 183
— *halepensis* 183
— × *holfordiana* 183
— *jeffreyi* 184
— *leucodermis* 184
— — 'Compact Gem' **91**, 184
— *montezumae* **95**, 184
— *monticola* 184
— *mugo* **101**, 184
— — 'Gnom' **90**, 184
— — 'Mops' **94**, 185
— — var *mugo* 185
— — var *pumilio* **89**, 185
— *muricata* **100**, 185
— *nigra* **89**, 185

Pinus nigra—contd.
— — var *caramanica* 185
— — var *cebennensis* 185
— — 'Hornibrookiana' **96**
— — var *maritima* 185
— — var *nigra* 185
— — 'Pygmaea' 185
— *parviflora* 185
— — 'Adcocks Dwarf' 186
— — 'Glanca' **87**, 186
— — 'Templehof' 186
— *patula* 186
— *peuce* 186
— *pinaster* 186
— *pinea* 186
— *ponderosa* 186
— *pumila* 187
— — 'Glauca' 187
— *radiata* 187
— — 'Aurea' 187
— *strobus* 187
— — 'Nana' 187
— *sylvestris* 187
— — 'Argentea Compacta' **92**,
        188
— — 'Aurea' **98**, 188
— — 'Beuvronensis' 188
— — 'Fastigiata' 188
— — 'Globosa Viridis' 188
— — 'Doone Valley' 188
— — 'Nana' 188
— — 'Watereri' **97**, 188
— *wallichiana* 188

Podocarpus 194
— *acutifolius* **113**, 194
— *alpinus* 195
— *andinus* 195
— *dacrydioides* 195
— *ferrugineus* 195
— *nivalis* 195
— *salignus* 195
— *spicatus* 195
— *totara* 195
— — 'Aurea' **114**, 196

Pseudolarix 188
— *amabilis* 189

Pseudotsuga 189
— *menziesii* 189
— — var *caesia* 190
— — 'Fletcheri' **99**, 190

Sciadopitys 190
— *verticillata* **102**, 190

Sequoia 199
— *sempervirens* 200
— — 'Adpressa' **109**, 200
— — 'Prostrata' **108**, 200

Sequoiadendron 200
— *giganteum* 201
— — 'Pendulum' 201
— — 'Pygmaeum' 201

Taxodium 201
— *ascendens* 201
— — 'Nutans' 201
— *distichum* 202

Taxus 122
— *baccata* 122
— — 'Adpressa' 122
— — 'Adpressa Variegata' 122
— — 'Amersfoort' 122
— — 'Aurea' 123
— — 'Dovastoniana' 123
— — 'Dovastonii Aurea' **3**, 123
— — 'Elegantissima' 123
— — 'Fastigiata' 123
— — 'Fastigiata Aureomarginata'
        123
— — 'Lutea' 123
— — 'Nutans' 123
— — 'Repandens' 123
— — 'Rushmore', *see* 'Amersfoort'
— — 'Semperaurea' **2**, 123
— — 'Standishii' 123
— — 'Washingtonii' 123
— *cuspidata* 124

Taxus cuspidata—contd.
—— 'Nana' 124
— × *media* 124
—— 'Hatfieldii' 124
—— 'Hicksii' 124
—— 'Thayerae' 124

Thuja 157
— *koraiensis* 158
— *occidentalis* 158
—— 'Alba' 158
—— 'Aurea' 158
—— 'Beaufort' 158
—— 'Caespitosa' **48**, 158
—— 'Columbia' 158
—— 'Ericoides' **37**, 158
—— 'Fastigiata' 159
—— 'Globosa' 159
—— 'Hetz Midget' 159
—— 'Holmstrup' 159
—— 'Little Gem' 159
—— 'Lutescens' **46**, 159
—— 'Ohlendorffii' 159
—— 'Rheingold' **53**, 159
—— 'Smaragd' 159
—— 'Vervaeneana' 160
—— 'Wansdyke Silver' 160
—— 'Wareana' 160
—— 'Wareana Lutescens', *see*
        'Lutescens'
—— 'Woodwardii' 160
— *orientalis* 160
—— 'Aurea Nana' **52**, 160
—— 'Beverleyensis' **50**, 160
—— 'Conspicua' **49**, 160

—— 'Filiformis Erecta' 160
—— 'Juniperioides' **51**, 160
—— 'Meldensis' 161
—— 'Rosedalis' **54**, 161
— *plicata* 161
—— 'Atrovirens' 161
—— 'Cuprea' 161
—— 'Hillieri' 161
—— 'Old Gold' **47**, 161
—— 'Rogersii' 161
—— 'Stoneham Gold' 161
—— 'Zebrina' 162

Thujopsis 162
— *dolabrata* 162
—— 'Aurea' 162
—— 'Nana' 162
—— 'Variegata' 162

Torreya 125
— *californica* 125
— *nucifera* **1**, 126

Tsuga 190
— *canadensis* 191
—— 'Aurea' 191
—— 'Bennett' **106**, 191
—— 'Cole' 191
—— 'Jeddeloh' **107**, 191
—— 'Minima' 192
—— 'Pendula' **105**, 192
— *caroliniana* 192
— *heterophylla* 192
— *mertensiana* 192
—— 'Argentea' **103**, 192
—— 'Glauca' 192